Education in the 80's:

CURRICULAR CHALLENGES

CURRICULAR CHALLENGES

Lois V. Edinger
Paul L. Houts
Dorothy V. Meyer
Editors

National Education Association
Washington, D.C.

Stock No. 3169-5-00 (paper)
        3170-9-00 (cloth)

Note

The opinions expressed in this publication should not be construed as representing the policy or position of the National Education Association. Materials published as part of the NEA Education in the 80's series are intended to be discussion documents for teachers who are concerned with specialized interests of the profession.

A portion of the proceeds from the sale of this book is being donated to the *Ole Sand Memorial Fund*.

Library of Congress Cataloging in Publication Data
Main entry under title:

Education in the 80's—curricular challenges.

  (Education in the 80's)
  Essays in memory of Ole Sand.
  Includes bibliographical references.
    Contents: Societal expectations for public education: Societal expectations for the American school . . . / Ralph W. Tyler. The democratic society and the American school / Edward J. Meade, Jr. — Teachers and students of the 80's: Students and student prototypes of the 80's / Lois V. Edinger — [etc.]
    1. Educational sociology—United States—Addresses, essays, lectures. 2. Politics and education—Addresses, essays, lectures. 3. School management and organization—United States—Addresses, essays, lectures. 4. Curriculum planning—United States—Addresses, essays, lectures.
I. Edinger, Lois V.   II. Houts, Paul L.   III. Meyer, Dorothy V.   IV. Sand, Ole.
V. Title: Education in the eighties—Curricular challenges.   IV. Series.
LC191.4.E38   370'.973   81–9437
ISBN 0–8106–3170–9   AACR2
ISBN 0–8106–3169–5 (pbk.)

Contents

OLE SAND

As we think about Ole Sand, we have many memories of his work and his effect on education. He stood for many things, not the least of which were the central role of the school in American society and the interdependence of school and society. He could not see one without the other, and he truly believed that the future of each was in the hands of both.

Ole Sand was an activist, long before the term achieved its popular status. He thought, he wrote, he spoke out, he participated in the affairs of society on the simple assumption that such was expected of any citizen of this nation. It is that memory of Ole Sand that led us to offer these essays.

The essays in this book were written by educators with varied backgrounds and diverse points of view. It is not by accident that this happened since our intent is that this collection of readings stimulate dialogue about education in the 80's. This dialogue should involve all those concerned with the future of education: the practitioners—both teachers and administrators, the academic community of students and faculty, citizens organizations, parent associations, and policy makers.

Ole Sand, in whose memory this book is presented, served as a catalyst, causing diverse groups of people to discuss educational issues and to listen to each other. He delighted in uncovering new issues and presenting them in both a serious and a humorous manner. He strove for a balance between the theoretical and the practical. We have sought to capture that spirit in the essays presented here.

The essays representing the personal views of the individual writers have been grouped under five broad categories: *Societal Expectations for Public Education, Teachers and Students of the 80's, The School Program: The Nature of the Curriculum for the 80's, The Politicalization of Education,* and *The Unfinished Agenda.*

Unlike the 60's and early 70's, when the excitement of new ideas and new programs, coupled with new sources of funding, thrust us forward in pursuit of new educational opportunities for all, we face the 80's with some trepidation. Declining enrollments force the closing of many public schools; reductions in force cause the unemployment and underemployment of teachers; the curtailment of funds limits the kinds of educational programs offered. As educators we are called upon to answer the sound of an uncertain trumpet—and the essays here address some of these uncertain sounds. While these essays are intended to be representative of the issues that need to be addressed as we view education in the 80's, we anticipate that other issues will be generated from discussions of these in classroom settings, open forums, town meetings, and study groups.

We acknowledge the help and support of the Ole Sand Memorial Fund Committee: Robert M. McClure, Paul L. Houts, Anna Hyer, Frances Quinto, and Thomas Sand. The Committee was most receptive when we first presented the idea of compiling a book of essays, and it has given us strong encouragement along the way. Special appreciation must go to the authors, many of whom were both personal and professional friends of Ole Sand, who contributed so willingly of their time and professional knowledge in preparing this series of essays.

The agenda for the *Schools for the 60's* gave us clear, fascinating, and exciting direction. The agenda for the *Schools for the 70's and Beyond* called upon us to make schools more humane. Today our society is uncertain; directions are unclear—and this, too, is reflected in our schools. It is imperative that we pause and consider in a profound way the issues that are before us. Thus, we present to you EDUCATION IN THE 80'S: CURRICULAR CHALLENGES.

Lois V. Edinger
Paul L. Houts
Dorothy V. Meyer

Part I

SOCIETAL EXPECTATIONS FOR PUBLIC EDUCATION

Are schools as we know them dying institutions? And by the end of this century will the demise be complete? Will the institutional-green coffin be buried and an appropriate tombstone raised? Could the stone well be engraved with Mark Twain's famous observation, "I never let my schooling interfere with my education"?

Ole Sand

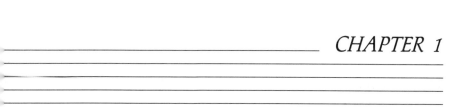

CHAPTER 1

Societal Expectations for the American School:
A Long View
Ralph W. Tyler

THE FUNCTIONS OF EDUCATION

Two functions of the educational system—socialization and social mobility—are found in all modern industrial nations, and a third—the development of self-realization—has become accepted in the United States. *Socialization* refers to the acquisition of the knowledge, skills, and attitudes required for effective participation in the society. It includes learning what is necessary to take part in the political life, in the economic life, and in the social institutions of the community. *Social mobility,* the change in family status from generation to generation, has been recognized as important since the days of the ancient Pharaohs when the sons of emperors were not permitted to assume the throne. The ancient Egyptians had learned that few sons of powerful rulers had developed the self-discipline required for effective leadership. They recruited vigorous rulers from families of lesser power. Since that time, many nations have obtained a significant part of their leadership from the children of families with less status, children who were reared to be responsible, energetic, and well-disciplined. The third function, *self-realization,* has received increasing interest from Americans as they have recognized the varieties of human potential to be found in the varied cultures of our society and the wide range of individual characteristics within each culture. This has led to a concern that children and youth be helped to attain their individual purposes and to realize their unique potentials, rather than to be trained to be like everyone else.

RESPONDING TO SOCIETAL EXPECTATIONS

The American educational system has been amazingly responsive to the demand for socialization. From a population of many ethnic, religious, and racial backgrounds, the system has helped produce citizens who maintain and constructively contribute to a democratic political order that is both stable and dynamic. For more than 200 years, this nation has been governed by the same political system, while all other large western nations have had two or more forms of state. During the 1860's the United States went through a terrible struggle to maintain the Union and the constitutional government, but the aftermath was a stronger nation, increasingly seeking liberty and justice for all.

The educational system has developed an intelligent and flexible labor force that is essential to an economy based on science and technology. The education of young people has been a major factor as the composition of the labor force has shifted enough to make it possible to provide an increasing amount of services when the need for labor to produce material goods is sharply declining. At the turn of the century, about 61 percent of the American labor force was unskilled; now this figure is less than 5 percent. As the demand for unskilled labor has declined, the opportunities for employment in health services, education services, social services, recreation, administration, accounting, science, and engineering have greatly increased. These occupations require primarily intellectual and social skills, in contrast to the emphasis on physical strength and manual dexterity characteristic of most of the occupations for which the demand is diminishing. Because of the large number of educated people in this country, there has been no serious lack of persons to take advantage of the shifting employment patterns.

Although the process of desegregation of schools, housing, and employment has not been without community conflicts, on the whole it is taking place peaceably. Opinion polls show clearly that the greater the amount of schooling a person has, the more likely s/he is to approve of equal treatment of all people, regardless of race, religion, or ethnic background; thus, the educational system appears to be contributing to community socialization.

In response to the expectation of social mobility, our educational system has supported the concept of an open society, and the educational opportunities it has provided have resulted in social mobility to an extent that is unprecedented in human history. From 1920 to 1960, approximately 50 percent of the American people moved up at least one step in social status, while only about 25 percent of them moved down.

There are few indications of the extent to which our educational system is helping individuals attain their own unique potentials. In most western nations this function is not seen as a responsibility of public education. Unique potential is recognized as important only for the elite. That American schools attempt to contribute to individual self-realization is indicated by their offering of elective courses and enrichment units, and by their provision of individual counselors. The biographies of some Americans and the testimony given 15 years later by those who participated in Project Talent during high school indicate that the schools have helped many persons pursue their individual interests and develop the abilities and talents that have helped them to achieve their individual goals.

ATTAINING UNIVERSAL LITERACY

In reviewing the expectations that society holds for the educational system, it is evident that the area of literacy has been considered the special responsibility of the school. When the Declaration of Independence was signed in 1776, historians estimate that about 15 percent of American adults were literate. Hunters and trappers did not need to read or write. Farmers did not need to be literate to fell the forests, plant the seeds, and harvest the crops in the rapidly expanding land. The relatively few educated leaders were concerned that the new nation would be isolated from civilization and provincial in its outlook; that its people would have no sense of history, no understanding of the progress made by humankind and of the problems encountered in the human quest for the meaning of life, and no vision of a civilized society and of the great potential of both human persons and social institutions. Universal literacy, the goal of the public schools, was seen as a means of overcoming narrowness of outlook, ignorance, and superstition.

The progress made over the next 200 years is indicated by the following facts. By 1918, when 2 million young men were tested as they were drafted into military service in World War I, 35 percent of them were literate. The tests of those inducted into military service in World War II showed nearly 55 percent to be literate. The most recent data from the National Assessment of Educational Progress show that more than 80 percent of 17-year-olds can read and comprehend the kind of prose used in typical American newspapers.[1] Most of the children who are not learning to read have parents who have had little or no education. However, it is encouraging to see from the national assessment reports that an increasing proportion of these children is learning to read. Although the goal of universal literacy has not yet been achieved, great progress has been made.

Taking the long view, it is clear that the American educational system has been amazingly responsive to societal expectations. Furthermore, the schools particularly have been responding to the ever-increasing demand for literacy. But now the educational system is encountering greater difficulty than in the past in meeting societal expectations. Two primary factors account for this difficulty. The particular requirements for socialization, social mobility, and self-realization are greater today than in earlier periods. During the past 20 years the out-of-school constructive learning experiences have been seriously reduced for a majority of American children and youth. Hence, at the present time there is great confusion among educational leaders, as well as among the public, over establishing the priorities of educational objectives, determining the extent of progress being made in reaching accepted goals, and identifying difficulties and problems that retard or prevent the attainment of these goals.

THE PRESENT AND FUTURE REQUIREMENTS

Political Socialization

The United States is committed to a democratic political system in which every citizen is both ruler and subject, and the knowledge, skills, and attitudes that citizens must develop in order to effectively participate in this type of political system are greater than those required by a political system in which a small group of leaders or a party has political control. In America, it is expected that every citizen will have learned to consider the common good—that is, the public interest—rather than being concerned only with her or his selfish interests. It is also expected that each citizen will have developed the skills and knowledge required to vote intelligently and to analyze and give support to legislation that appears to promote the public interest. This is a more difficult educational task than the one faced by an authoritarian society that seeks to teach its citizens both to appreciate the contribution being made by the political regime and to support the political leaders in ways appropriate for the citizens' positions in the society. The task in America has become increasingly difficult as our nation has become both urbanized and deeply enmeshed in the activities, problems, and conflicts of other nations with whom we have a multitude of political, economic, and social relationships. Furthermore, pressures brought to bear on our political system by the many special interest groups are neither easily recognized nor likely to be treated objectively because all citizens have special interests and find it difficult to support as their primary concern the public interest. For 25 years our attention has been focused on group and individual rights, to the neglect of social responsibilities. Finally, our political system is the oldest in the western world, and most citizens take it for granted, lacking deep appreciation of its value and showing little concern for its maintenance and improvement.

Under these circumstances it is not surprising to find that the national assessment results indicate that many of our young people do not understand why governments are necessary and what the particular characteristics of our government are. Many 17-year-olds do not know what their civic responsibilities are, and nearly half do not believe in the ideals embodied in the Bill of Rights. This problem is also indicated by the results of the Evaluation of Educational Achievement; with regard to civic knowledge and attitudes, American youth stood in the lowest third of the 10 nations tested, while the youth of the Federal Republic of Germany were at the top.[2] I suspect that some of this difference can be accounted for by the fact that the political system of West Germany is relatively new. American youth were probably much more aware of their government and its ideals and values in 1800 when the nation was in its infancy.

Economic Socialization

The rapid changes taking place in this country in the production and distribution of goods and services have greatly affected the particular knowledge, skills, and attitudes required of those who participate in production. In recent years science and technology have joined to make this rate of change increasingly rapid. Hence, workers in all fields are expected to develop the ability to adapt themselves to new practices in existing occupations or to entirely new occupations. These changes place a relatively new demand on educational systems in modern *industrialized* nations. Furthermore, machines are rapidly replacing human beings in the production of material goods, while the demand for services like health care has so increased that those employed in such service areas represent nearly two-thirds of the labor force. This trend places great pressure on the schools to help young people develop the intellectual and social skills required for the service occupations. In brief, the occupational education expected in a modern industrialized nation like the United States is far different from that in an agricultural society, which we largely were before World War I.

Economic socialization includes more than education for production. American citizens also need to learn what is necessary for the wise consumption of limited resources. As the purchasing power of families increases, the traditional constraints on consumption arising from relative poverty are loosened, and wasteful, harmful, and short-sighted consumption practices increase unless education is effective in developing the necessary understanding, disposition, and skills.

There is also a relatively new factor in wise consumption. If the American people wanted only food, clothing, and shelter, a major fraction of the population would be unemployed because these goods can be produced by a small part of our labor force. The desire and the willingness to pay for health, education, and recreation (including art, music, literature, sports, and the like) create the demand that enables the economy to shift its patterns of production to take advantage of the greater efficiency of technology.

The consumer education courses that were constructed in the 20's and 30's emphasized the development of the abilities required to make choices among material products, using information about the serviceable qualities and relative costs of these goods. The chief problem for consumers of that period was believed to be their obtaining useful products at the lowest prices commensurate with necessary quality. Few of these courses dealt with the problems involved in making wise choices among goods and services that furnish nonmaterial values: for example, the aesthetic values in music, art, and drama; the recreational values in sports; the personal and social values in various educational opportunities; the health values in different forms of health and medical programs. At most, English courses sought to develop an appreciation for literature that could afford continuing meaning and satisfaction to the reader, and a small number of courses devoted to motion picture appreciation aimed to help students make wise choices in the movies they viewed.

Now that a majority of the labor force is engaged in service occupations, the range of possible choices for the consumer is increasing greatly. Hence, this realignment of economic functions opens up a whole new area of consumer education and requires the development of relevant objectives and learning experiences. The wise choice of these services is profoundly important in the development both of individuals and of our culture. Choices of literature, art, music, recreation, leisure time, educational opportunities, health services, and contributing social services have a great deal to do with the quality of life.

Community Socialization

The expectation that, through education, people will learn to participate peacefully, constructively, and humanely in the family and in the social institutions and organizations of the community is also more demanding today than it was in earlier years. Two hundred years ago communities were smaller and more homogeneous. Differences in race, religion, and ethnic background were not as sharply evident in the routine interactions in small towns and rural areas. The conflicts that arose in areas where new immigrants were settling were not characteristic of much of the country.

Today, immigration, both legal and illegal, along with migration of poor families from rural areas to urban centers, continues to stimulate conflicts. Furthermore, the multiplication of communication channels makes the stresses and strains within communities more widely known. The civil rights movement has broadened the definition of neighbor and has established ideals for equality of opportunity that were not heretofore generally accepted. For these reasons, the socialization required for constructive community participation is more difficult, and more necessary, now than ever before.

Social Mobility

During the past 60 years, social mobility in the United States reached a level undreamed of by earlier generations. This mobility was accounted for largely by two factors: (1) our economic system required fewer and fewer unskilled workers and at the same time increased its demands for professional and administrative services; (2) our educational system responded by helping large numbers of young people acquire the skills, knowledge, and attitudes needed to take advantage of these new employment opportunities. In 1920, professional and managerial occupations represented about 5 percent of the labor force; now nearly 20 percent are so employed. In 1920, unskilled and semiskilled labor made up half the labor force; now they comprise only 15 percent.

As this nation continues its economic development, there will, no doubt, be further increases in the proportion of workers who are professional, semiprofessional, and managerial, but we are likely to approach a plateau; at that point, increases in social status will occur primarily as workers excel both occupationally and in community service and as they assume greater responsibilities within the same occupation or within a voluntary organization. Obviously, this relatively new kind of social mobility depends heavily on education—that is, on learning skills, knowledge, and attitudes, and on acquiring interests and values that provide the vision and the ability requisite to increased social status. But this task may prove more difficult for our educational system than helping persons become competent to perform effectively in the next level job.

Self-Realization

A modern industrial society furnishes many more avenues for self-realization than were available in the small towns and rural areas of the past; but it also creates more pressures for conformity. Furthermore, folklore, the mass media, and many educators convey stereotypes of occupations, social performance, and "normal persons" that inhibit the desire and effort to achieve self-fulfillment. In occupational education, for example, emphasis is placed on each occupation's typical activities and skills, rather than on perceiving that most occupations permit a wide range of emphases, ways of performing effectively, and styles of life. Too often, education is viewed as fitting persons into their niches rather than as opening up an increasing range of options for their lives. Even guidance counselors often think of themselves as helping students narrow their educational and occupational choices rather than increase them.

As we become more conscious of the kinds of human potential that can be realized through learning about the world, about ourselves, and about the variety of contributions that persons can make, we should be able to clarify the educational goals appropriate for self-realization. Then will come increasing exploration of ways the educational system can help individuals attain these goals.

This brief review of the requirements to meet societal expectations of education today and in the future shows clearly that these demands are greater than they have been in the past. The American educational system is expected to do much more now than ever before.

THE EROSION OF OUT-OF-SCHOOL EDUCATION

I have been discussing the societal expectations for the educational system, recognizing that the school is only part of the total educational system. As children each of us probably learned more outside the school than we did within it. The home, the religious institutions, the playgrounds, the press, the employment situations, and the other institutions outside the schoolroom furnished experiences that helped us to learn basic character traits, commitment to social values, respect for authority, habits of work, and the like that are essential to productive and constructive living.

Research has shown that a very important factor accounting for some of the school learning problems is the lack of constructive learning experiences in the home.[3] At one time, this type of home situation was found largely among poor families, those families with only one adult, and those families in which the parents were either uneducated or from a very different culture.

Now there are increasing numbers of homes in which constructive learning experiences are not provided (1) because both parents are at work and no provision has been made for supervision of the children when they return from school, and (2) because television viewing has pre-empted much of the time parents used to devote to instructing their children. In 1979, 59 percent of the mothers of school-age children were in the labor force as compared to 26 percent in 1960. When a national sample of children from 10 to 14 years of age was studied by Schramm, Lyle, and Parker, they found that the average child spends 1,500 hours per year viewing television and only 1,100 hours per year in school.[4] The programs most popular with children were largely entertainment, thus distracting them from study and not contributing to habits involving effort to accomplish something constructive.

Totalitarian countries provide adult supervision of children throughout their waking hours because their leaders understand the importance of out-of-school time in shaping the child. As a nation we are committed to preserving the opportunities for parents to guide their own children, but we cannot afford to see this home responsibility neglected.

Another important area of out-of-school learning is the employment situation. The school, together with the home, can help young people develop habits of punctuality and industry. The school can help develop understanding of the world of work, the functions of each sector, and the kind of tasks carried on. But the school cannot develop the occupational skills, the sense of responsibility, and the attitudes required in particular work situations. At present many young people experience a serious gap as they make the transition from school to work. The seriousness of the problem is not understood in many localities; yet, it is at the local level where the youth are, where the jobs must be found, and where the schools are. To attack this problem will usually require the collaborative effort of the local school, employers, unions, and civic leaders. Until this problem is dealt with effectively, societal expectations with regard to occupational education will not be met.

There are other community institutions, organizations, and individuals that can help in providing the educational experiences needed to ensure adequate out-of-school learning. One way to stimulate communities to rebuild these opportunities for learning is to establish educational councils the function of which is to survey the out-of-school educational opportunities in the community and to publicize deficiencies that can be remedied by voluntary organizational efforts. It is not likely that we can obtain increases in tax support for youth service, but we can emulate the efforts of Jane Addams who saw the children of immigrants failing to learn in the Chicago schools because they lacked the supportive home background. Arousing the interest and securing the financial backing of city residents, she was able to establish Hull House as a substitute for the learning environment provided by middle-class American homes. College students and other educated persons in the city spent afternoons and evenings in the settlement house tutoring and serving in other ways as parent substitutes. The difficulties the children of immigrants encountered in learning what the schools were teaching were greatly lessened by settlement houses in Chicago, New York, Boston, and Philadelphia.

Certainly the public today needs to understand that society's increasing expectations of education cannot be met in the 1,100 hours per year that children and youth spend in schools.

IN SUMMARY

The societal expectations of the American educational system are far greater today than ever before; yet, at the same time, the constructive learning opportunities outside the schools are diminishing. This presents a critical, but not insoluble, situation. There are greater resources for learning in America than during any previous period. Community leaders working with the schools and with the other social institutions can mobilize these resources to increase the educational effectiveness of our nation.

REFERENCES

1. The National Assessment of Educational Progress, 1860 Lincoln Street, Denver, Colorado, 1980.

2. International Association for the Evaluation of Educational Achievement. *International Studies in Evaluation*. New York: John Wiley; Stockholm: Alqvist & Wiksell, 1973. Six volumes.

3. Bronfenbrenner, Urie. *The Ecology of Human Development*. Cambridge, Mass.: Harvard University Press, 1979. Chapter 8.

4. Schramm, Wilburt; Lyle, Jack; and Parker, Edwin B. *Television in the Lives of Our Children*. Palo Alto, Calif.: Stanford University Press, 1961.

CHAPTER 2

The Democratic Society and the American School
Edward J. Meade, Jr.

The American society and the American school depend on and reinforce each other. Public schools were created in this country to educate the young in order that they would become full participants in American life. Perhaps this interdependent relationship and this educational mission were most visible during the years from just before the turn of the 1900's until shortly after mid-century. During that time, the American school—public, free, and found in almost every community —stood as a beacon of hope and opportunity, and as the means of achieving much of the American dream. For many of our fellow citizens who went to school during this period, the American school delivered on its promise, and, as a result, countless numbers entered fully into the mainstream of American life, equipped to enrich and be enriched by this nation and its society. However, for those disadvantaged by poverty, discrimination, neglect, or handicap, the dream was largely unfulfilled —a fact that became alarmingly apparent during the past quarter century.

Still, the emergence of the American public school, and its continuing evolution, is looked upon by many observers, especially those from other countries, as one of this nation's greatest achievements. Since public education began in this country, its quantitative and qualitative growth has been nothing short of phenomenal. Few American neighborhoods are without their public school buildings; they are as common to our communities as our homes, our shops, and our workplaces. Just as we have more and more schools, we have more and more schooling. Once the average number of years in school for all children was but a handful of years; today it is more like 12 or more for many of them. What could be learned in school was once limited to a few subjects; today the curriculum is much richer and, in spite of some excesses here and there, more responsive overall to the needs of pupils and of society. Once the range of pupils served by the public schools was limited; today's schools have become more culturally, socially, and racially diverse, serving those of varying age levels, abilities, and interests, and, recently, including handicapped children in mainstream classrooms. Further, the individual school and the local community school district, once fully dependent on local support, now get more help from the state and the federal governments.

Much more can be said about the success of the American school in terms of its capacities, its diversity, and its outcomes. Suffice it to say that, in many ways, it is truly remarkable, and markedly so, when contrasted with forms and systems of public education in many other countries. While some of these systems may appear superior in certain ways—for example, in their emphasis on educating the academically talented—few can match the American system in its attempt to educate everyone for so long and in so many ways, and in its record of succeeding so often.

Over time, the American people came to believe that the American school could do just about anything that was asked of it or that it tried to do. Often this faith was justified, as shown by the following two examples. At the turn of the century, city schools embraced thousands of European immigrants, and, despite the barriers of different languages and cultures, the schools worked hand-in-hand with these new Americans, and they learned. Second, in other areas, and particularly in the more remote rural communities and small towns, the local school became the locus for the community's cultural and social life, all in addition to fulfilling its educational mission.

The American school responded time and time again to the society's needs, expectations, and demands. It provided support on the home front when the nation went to war; it responded in times of disasters, whether they were economic depressions caused by human acts or physical disasters caused by nature; it nurtured minds as it was expected to do, but it nurtured bodies as well. These responses and others justified the faith Americans had in the public school. In fact, such responses and the consequent increase of faith in the public school led the public to make more and more demands on it. As long as the school could get the resources to add to what it already was doing and as long as the school and the public's faith in it were not seriously questioned, the American school continued to deliver. Whether it was providing a hot lunch in the middle of the school day; training drivers for America's growing system of roads and highways; teaching future farmers, latheworkers, and secretaries along with the college-bound, from budding poets to scientific scholars; or developing athletes and performing artists, the school responded, willingly and successfully.

The American public school has been one of the most responsive public institutions created by this nation. Its adaptability for much of its history earned it a solid reputation with the public who supported it and who were served by it. Indeed, the American school was so respected that it took the traumas of our society over the past 25 or so years to enable us to see more clearly the American school in the fuller context of this nation and its communities, and not as something sacred, above and beyond the maelstrom of American social, economic, and political life.

This fall from grace is not surprising. In some ways it should be welcomed because the American school is hardly perfect. After all, what public institution is? Clearly there have been instances when the school overresponded. Over its history, it pulled, stretched, and expanded itself more often than it ever contracted. Rarely did the school push society to seek other ways and means to deal with something asked of it by the public; more often it changed and adapted itself, however imperfectly, to whatever it was asked to do. As a result, many Americans came to believe that the American school could somehow do almost anything it was asked to do—especially in earlier times of growth and of plenty. And for those it did not serve, their voices were not heard and their needs not met.

There are differences of opinion about when and why the American attitude toward the public school changed. Let us leave it to the historians to set the record straight. Still, the public school and the public's faith in it have changed. Events occurring in and out of education over the past 25 years have raised important questions about the role of the American school. During this span of years, the public school had to deal with the largest growth and perhaps the greatest changes in its history. Given the baby boom of the 1950's, the long-needed civil rights actions of the 1960's, and the excesses of government and the escalating material consumption of the public in the 1970's, the capacity of the school was tested as perhaps never before. The result certainly was not total failure. Time and time again during this period the school showed itself to be flexible and responsive. Sometimes, however, it failed to respond, or, at least, it did not respond quickly enough. And in some areas the school continued to be too responsive, causing it to give short shrift to more important things that it should have been doing because it could do them better than other institutions. Perhaps, during this period more than at any other time, a larger issue emerged, not necessarily for the first time but more sharply and realistically than before. That issue takes somewhat the form of the following question:

> *How can the American school ensure equal educational opportunities for all Americans regardless of their race, sex, culture, health, handicap, or age, and provide an equitable and useful education for each that will permit and nurture literacy and individual growth and that will also assure that each can effectively participate in the commerce of the nation and the world and in the governance of the American democracy?*

In itself, that question is a sufficient challenge. However, finding an answer—whatever the answer might be—is made more challenging because it is increasingly clear in this day and age that the question must be answered within a context of limits, and not one of growth. The facts are now before us—the population is stabilizing and aging; in many communities, demands for public services other than education are more pressing; physical and financial resources are increasingly limited; the overall economy of the nation is strained; and the national political and social climate is more and more turbulent and diverse. Clearly the public school will not be able to respond to whatever demands it should in the ways, or to the extent, that it did in the past.

Equally important as the context of limits is the context of faith in which the American school finds itself today. Events over the past quarter century have substantially affected the public's confidence in the school. For example, there have been instances in which schools were slow to respond to change, often because their communities resisted the change as well. No other illustration, perhaps, is as dramatic as that of school desegregation. From the time of the landmark Supreme Court decision in 1954 until today, this matter has caused differences, difficulties, and controversy. The troubles and turmoil that have been associated with school desegregation in all parts of the nation have contributed to an erosion of public faith in the American school. Other civil rights issues of more recent vintage, such as those related to sex and to physical and mental handicaps, have had a similar effect. This is not to say that issues of human and civil rights are not matters for the school to champion; in fact, quite the reverse must be the case. Rather, it is that

26

issues of this kind have revealed frailties in the capacity of the school to deal with them effectively.

Still another set of circumstances has further contributed to erosion of faith in the school. These circumstances relate, on the one hand, to the high expectations for the school as held by society and, on the other hand, to the capacity of the school to educate pupils who are both culturally and racially different and differently disadvantaged from the poor pupils of the past whom the school seemed to have served well. No longer can society and school rely on the circumstances of earlier times when pupils dropping out of school could easily enter an eager and receptive job market, or when high levels of pupil motivation and of community and family support enabled pupils to bridge the difference between their circumstances and backgrounds and those of the school. The issue is not whether or not the school is at fault today, or even whoever else is at fault. Instead, these changing realities simply help to explain why public faith in the American school has ebbed.

There are other factors that must be taken into account regarding the answer to the question that I raised earlier about the mission of the school today and in the future. Some of these factors are already visible and powerful. Clearly, one of them is the hand of government—district, state, and federal—which is determining more strongly than ever before how the American school addresses the question. Certainly, the wave of state and federal court decisions about a variety of human and civil rights issues has dramatically affected how the question can be answered. Further, the extent of financial and policy dependence of the school on the state and federal governments, for better or worse, is a fact of life. But then it is also a fact of life for most public service agencies in any local community, and no doubt it will continue for some time to come.

Another factor today can be seen and heard in the debates and commentary and in the activities that focus on the objectives of the school. Such talk and activity are not novel, but much of today's approach may be. In past years, changing the objectives of the school often meant adding to them. That luxury does not seem to be present any longer. There are strong moves today to change educational objectives, not only by adding but also by subtracting or contracting. Some persons want the American school to relate more closely to the jobs to be filled by the American labor force. Others want the objectives to be less related to vocations and jobs and more related to intellectual development. Still others want education to be more individualized or more closely tailored to the needs of the students, whether they are handicapped, disadvantaged, gifted, or average. Any observer of the American school today could easily add other examples. The point is that it is in the debates about the objectives for the American school that one may find the seeds of answers to the central question that I raised earlier.

As suggested earlier, government's role in public education, especially at the federal and state levels in recent years, cannot help but affect how the mission of the school is to be determined. Certainly, the "how" has already been greatly influenced, particularly through the courts and the federal government, over the past 25 or so years; laws and programs mandate more *equality* and *equity* as necessary conditions for schooling if a school is to be public in its nature and in its support.

Government at all levels also determines the amount of resources available for public education, at least as far as financial resources are concerned. With today's economic realities and with those projected for the future, it is clear that such resources will be limited. Further, most funding at the federal and state levels will continue to be appropriated largely to assure equality and equity in the schools because those are the principles that undergird such appropriations.

How this situation has affected and will further affect the public's faith in the American school is open to speculation. Most observers would agree that our public education system today is more equitable than in the past, that it provides more access, and more equal access at that, and that it is more sensitive to individual rights. The debates occur when issues of educational objectives and the quality of the schooling proposed to deal with them are raised.

Nowhere are these issues of purpose and quality more visible and audible than in some of the school-based movements that are currently marching under various banners labeled as "back-to-basics," "fundamentals for learning," "essential skills," "basic competencies," "humanistic education," "education for the future," and others. While no two movements are the same, each represents an attempt to define and order more clearly and sharply the mission of the school. Often proponents of one or another of these movements demand that the school return to the kind of purpose their banner implies; they seem to be saying that the school is presently not serving this purpose, that it is doing more than it should be, and that much of the "more" is less important and should be eliminated. On the other hand, others declare that the school has never left the mission that these forces demand, implying that the problem is more one of emphasis than one requiring change or elimination.

Regardless of these two views and others like them, the public seeks clarity. It wants to know what the school can do best in response to the demands placed on it; it wants to know what the school can be certain to deliver that no other institution can. The public's faith, or lack of faith, in the school and the level of that faith will be shaped by the resolution of concerns of this nature.

In determining what the role of the school should be, I would remind us of the central question that I cited earlier. In it, three broad objectives emerge about which, I believe, there is general agreement: (1) literacy and individual growth, (2) participation in the commerce of the nation and the world, and (3) effective participation in the governance of the American democracy. Each is as traditional as it is contemporary or futuristic. But, alas, each is general and broad. And it is in the further definition of each wherein lies not only the controversy but also the challenge and the opportunity for the people to decide democratically and with wisdom and common sense what each of these objectives should encompass.

Time and space do not permit more than a brief comment on each of these three objectives. It is my contention, however, that the record of performance of the school with respect to each is not similar, and, in fact, for one of them, it has been well below what it will need to be in the future. I refer to the third of these objectives: education for effective participation in the governance of the American democracy. Further, when this one objective is compared to the other two, it has received less attention and, as a result, less solid thinking, discussion, and effort.

This is not to say that all is well with respect to the two other objectives: literacy and individual growth, and participation in the workplace. That is hardly the case for either of them. Still, the public and the schools seem more comfortable and, in some ways, better able to deal with those two objectives than with the third—civic competence and citizen participation.

In the area of literacy and individual growth, there is first the matter of nurturing the innate skills, abilities, and personal interests of the individual. Few would quarrel with the development of basic skills and literacy in thinking, reading, writing, computation, aesthetics, the arts, and the sciences. We need to have our individual potentials along these lines tapped and nurtured simply to prepare us to live in and be part of a society. We also each need to be exposed—early and well—to a wide variety of subjects so that we can apply our learned literacies to the choices we make about what interests us over the course of our lives. Later in the process, the school should further nurture and add knowledge about those interests that we select. Throughout all of schooling, we need to bear in mind that in this instance the goal is to develop individual literacy and basic competence, and to enhance life, individually and collectively.

The second objective—participation in the commerce of the nation and the world—relies substantially on the basic skills and literacies noted above, and, as a result, many of them need to be developed and honed in useful and practical ways. We also need to add to them knowledge and attitudes about working in general and about kinds of work in particular. And, somehow, but not of itself or within itself, the school has to help students experience work before each of them commits himself or herself to the marketplace.

Obviously, the above treatment of these two objectives for the school is altogether too brief and certainly subject to all kinds of questions. Suffice it to say that, to my way of thinking, each, at least in the general sense, is a primary and fundamental purpose for the school. I will say no more about either because I want to attend to the third, and equally primary, objective of education—effective participation in the governance of the American democracy.

This objective is part and parcel of American life and, therefore, of the American school. The very functioning of our nation requires an educated and participating citizenry. Our society could not long continue to be what it intends to be if its schools did not have civic competence and citizen participation among its primary objectives. Simply to educate and train interested and competent persons and workers is not sufficient for a democracy such as ours.

It could be argued that this objective is alive and well and already strongly in place in the American school. A look at the school program attests to its presence. The American school has curriculums under various labels designed to meet this objective: civics, citizenship education, law-related education, and social studies, to name a few. In addition, the American school prides itself on internal activities—e.g., student government; student newsletters; procedures that allow the participation of parents, teachers, students, and others in its affairs—that give expression to citizen participation in the democratic society.

My major concern is not that any or all of these curriculums and activities are necessarily good or bad, adequate or not. Rather, my concern arises for other reasons. First, today in almost all of our communities, in most of our states, and also at the national level, there are concerted efforts to improve the American school. That is as it should be. However, most of these efforts are aimed primarily at one or both of the other objectives I cited earlier. All of us are concerned about the school's performance in relation to basic education and about its capacity to prepare students for work. Still, in our zeal to improve the school along these lines, we often overlook the third and equally important mission of civic competence and citizen participation.

No matter what the objective of our efforts to improve the school —to undergird the development of the "basic" skills, to develop a student's capacity to think, to nurture a student's interests, to help a student find and fill a job, or to broaden a student's career opportunities —we cannot lose sight of the fact that our society expects and needs each person to be a participating citizen in the democracy. We cannot allow that mission to take second place or, worse, to be ignored, even if benignly.

Ours is a nation of laws—laws that give to each of us rights and, consequently, individual and collective responsibilities to assure that our rights and those of others will be maintained. The nurturing of the self and the preparing of the worker do not necessarily produce an informed and participating citizen. At the very least, we need to understand that along with the skills and literacies necessary for one to know, to think, to create, and to work are those necessary for one to participate effectively in the governance of society.

This mission takes on more importance as one looks at the present and to the future of American society. Our society has become diverse and complex, and it will only become more so. For example, our systems of communication and information bring us more knowledge about more matters more rapidly and vividly than ever before, and so they will in the future. Events, issues, knowledge, and views are communicated to each of us in overwhelming quantity and diversity, whether we are prepared to deal with them or not. In the same fashion and conversely, these same communication and information services mold opinions and attitudes almost as if the public has already so decided. It is not such an overstatement to claim that in the future the hallmark of participatory democracy in America—the town meeting—will not be a meeting of the citizens at large but rather a meeting of a small number of pollsters and media agencies acting, if you will, as a surrogate for the public and without its sanction.

The increased pluralism of our society is easily seen today, especially in and around schools. More than ever, perhaps, various special interest groups are making their views, needs, and demands known, and are seeking to have them met by the school. For good and often historical reasons, many of these groups have reason to doubt the school's willingness and capacity to meet these needs. As a result, their demands are made in ways that make compromise with other and equally justified demands and needs difficult. But the essence of democracy, in part at least, is effective compromise—the greatest good for the greatest number—short of a tyranny of the majority. We rely heavily on our judicial system as a safeguard against such a tyranny. Still, the judiciary cannot and should not resolve all conflicts. Resolving such matters in the school and in society at large calls for an informed citizenry skilled in participatory governance. Indeed, the strength of the democracy we seek rests, to a substantial degree, on the capacity and ability of each citizen to understand the issues of the present and the future, and to participate effectively with fellow citizens to resolve these issues. In that way, the decisions reached and the civic harmony achieved will be of and by the people, and for them as well.

If our citizens do not receive the training and knowledge necessary, and if they subsequently do not become actively involved in our democracy, governance could increasingly become the sole responsibility of those representatives we elect and appoint to our legislative and executive bodies—but without the foundation of the citizenry at large. Representative democracy, as we want it to be, calls for participating citizens, not simply for voters who elect others. In fact, the very keystone of our democracy is the individual citizen who is capable of participating in the decisions that govern each and all.

If future projections are anywhere near accurate, American citizens will need to be all the more knowledgeable and active in government at all levels if we expect to hold fast to the democratic principles that undergird our nation, our states, and our communities. As our lives become more complex and more interrelated, all of us will need to know and to think more about civic responsibility, and to become more active in our civic life so that better decisions are made to guide the course of our individual lives and that of our society. If we do not, we stand the chance of having our future determined for us, and not by and with us —a sad fate for a people who have chosen to have a society such as ours.

In short, our society demands that its people—each and every one of us—strengthen and not weaken democracy. To do so, our society expects and should demand that its schools educate and nurture its young in such ways that each of them will be prepared and committed to participate actively in its affairs of government and of law. If we are free and if we wish to remain so, each of us must be competent to participate equally and effectively as citizens. To my way of thinking, there is no more noble or challenging mission for the American school now, and for as long as this nation exists, than that of preparing its students to participate competently in the American democracy. Indeed, the very existence of our society as we want it to be depends, in large measure, on the American school's fulfilling this mission successfully.

Part II

TEACHERS AND STUDENTS OF THE 80's

It is one thing for a teacher to be elderly; it is quite another for a teacher to be obsolete, since the most powerful obsolescence comes from within, not from without.

But education is more than teachers—and the death of old institutions will bring many changes to other areas as well. Emphasis will shift, for example, from the group to the individual. Milk can be homogenized, but not children. We cannot pour 20 eight-year-olds into a classroom and expect them all to do the same thing or, more important, want to do the same thing.

Ole Sand

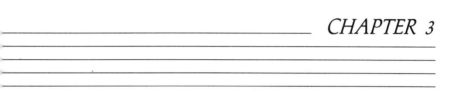

CHAPTER 3

Students and Student Prototypes of the 80's

Lois V. Edinger

Another article on students? The literature is replete with discussions of students, of how to identify and meet their needs, interests, and abilities. We already have more knowledge about students than we use. And why students of the 80's? Will they be so different from students of the past? Will there be a new breed of students in the 80's?

Student populations have been given labels in recent decades: the Quiet Generation of the 50's; the Protest (or Turbulent) Generation of the 60's; the "Relevancy" Generation of the 70's. If there is a new breed of students in the 80's, what will the label be?

As the decade of the 70's drew to a close, we saw the unrest and questioning of the earlier years resulting, more often than not, in vandalism, violence, and absenteeism. Finding appropriate solutions to continuing problems will require substantial energy and effort in the 80's. Simply applying more of the same treatment to the students who are opting out in those ways is not a solution.

Another condition that will make things different for students in the 80's is that there will be fewer of them. On the one hand, this may be an advantage for those who are in the public schools. On the other hand, it may not if the public continues its flirtation with alternative nonpublic schools. Resources may be decreased, thereby reducing or eliminating needed programs in the public schools.

While it is important to consider the conditions set forth above in discussing students in the 80's, there is, I believe, a far more significant consideration: the increasing demands on the school to deal with students as certain targeted populations. We have always done some of this in the schools, haven't we? We speak so glibly of below average, slow, average, above average, and accelerated groups of students that we are almost persuaded that these are absolutes.

In such a labeling process, schools are increasingly forced to give attention to both ends of the continuum. There is a tendency to overlook the great number of students whose only lament might be that they are "average" or "normal," or that, as some would say, they fit the organizational prototype. They play by the rules of the school, do their work (most of the time), don't get into serious trouble, have none of the "mandated special needs" to be met in the school program, and may even still give credence to the American dream that if you go to school and get an education, you can move up the social ladder and/or be a "better" person. They tend to conform to bureaucratic expectations and, hence, are seen as nondeviant. A typical bureaucrat, therefore, assumes that their needs are being met through the school organization.

A more useful typology than that given above has been utilized in the recent Carnegie Foundation report *Giving Youth a Better Chance: Options for Education, Work, and Service*. In that report, the following groups are identified:

1. *The Advantaged:* young persons who are from families in the top two-thirds of the income range and who finish high school.

2. *The Financially Disadvantaged:* young persons in the bottom one-third of the income range who finish high school but who, in doing so, may impose a financial hardship on their families and whose attendance in college does impose such a hardship.

3. *The Socially Deprived:* young persons who do not finish high school for reasons of social circumstances (family and community deprivations and social prejudices).

4. *The Personally Deprived:* young persons who do not finish high school for reasons of personal circumstances (mental, physical, or psychological disabilities).

5. *The Opt-outs:* young persons who do not choose to participate in the established educational or academic institutions of society for reasons of personal choice or philosophical orientation.[1]

Such a typology is quite to my liking as we move into the 80's because I believe it allows for flexibility in dealing with individuals and their needs; however, I think it may be difficult for the schools to utilize fully this typology in dealing with students. I say this because we are now operating under certain mandates that have been established by courts and/or legislative bodies or that have been imposed by certain pressure groups within society—mandates that force the schools to deal with students in quite a different fashion.

One of the certainties of the 80's is that schools will be required to deal with bureaucratically imposed programs designed to give mandated special treatment to targeted groups in the school. In no way do I mean to imply that the groups so targeted are not deserving of special treatment. The question is simply this: Can schools do all that is demanded of them *and* meet the needs of untargeted populations?

Neither is the statement above intended to be unduly critical of schools. The school as an organization responds the way any organization responds; it deals with prototypes, not individuals. Can the organization respond effectively to so many mandated programs, none of which fits the traditional prototype program?

Now, having raised the issue of mandated special treatment for groups of students, it is necessary to identify such groups. These groups fall under two broad categories:

1. Groups of students singled out for mandated special treatment by court action and/or legislation.

2. Groups of students who, because of growing numbers, are apt to attract strong pressure groups advocating special treatment. Such advocacy may lead to mandated action, but even without that, the increasing pressure within a community or state will force the schools to respond.

In the space of this essay, one can deal with only a few examples under each category. We are familiar with programs already under way for students who fall into the first of these categories. Specific treatment within educational institutions for handicapped persons has been mandated. Schools are required under the law to provide programs for persons who exhibit any of the nine handicapping conditions identified in the law: (1) deaf, (2) hard of hearing, (3) mentally retarded, (4) orthopedically impaired, (5) other health impaired, (6) seriously emotionally disturbed, (7) specific learning disability, (8) speech impaired, and (9) visually handicapped.

Approximately 12 percent of the population in the United States between the ages of 3 and 21 have a handicap as defined under the law. It is estimated that approximately 8 million handicapped young persons had been generally neglected in the formal educational setting prior to the passage of PL 94-142, The Education for All Handicapped Children Act. It is not difficult to see the reason for mandated special treatment under these circumstances.

Students with handicapping conditions will continue to receive special treatment in the 80's. The major concerns of the schools will be to provide even more appropriate individualized programs with continuous progress reporting and to find appropriate ways of meeting competency test requirements for these youngsters. It can hardly be educationally sound to place handicapped students in regular classrooms and then fail them or deny them diplomas because of their failure on standardized competency tests when they have met the requirements of the individualized programs designed for them.

The implications of educating this targeted group of students in regular classrooms are enormous. All educational personnel will need to have some understanding of these students and their special needs. Overcrowding must be eliminated and class size reduced to allow for the personal relationships needed; educational settings will need to be changed to allow for greater flexibility in learning environments. Whether these changes occur or not, the fact that schools are mandated to provide for the handicapped will preoccupy the system, either in the doing of it or in the attempt to show that the requirements of the law are being met.

While a good many people have some knowledge of the legislation requiring programs for the handicapped in regular classrooms, not so many are aware of a Supreme Court decision [*Lau v. Nichols* 414 U.S. 563 (1974)] that requires schools to provide bilingual–bicultural education. This is another example of mandated treatment of students that will continue in the 80's. While the number of handicapped persons will probably not increase substantially over projections given, the number of non-English-speaking students is already increasing rapidly. For example, the number of Hispanic Americans is growing more rapidly than any other major segment of population in the United States. It is estimated that this group is becoming the largest minority in the country; target dates for when it will pass blacks as the largest minority range from 1982 to 2000. As of March 1978, official census figures listed 24.8 million blacks and 12.0 million Hispanic Americans.[2] However, the National Council of La Raza estimates the number at 16 million, and this does not include undocumented aliens and over 3 million residents of Puerto Rico.[3] No longer are Hispanic Americans concentrated along the

Southwest border and in Miami and New York City; 18 states, including states along the eastern coast, have large concentrations of Hispanic Americans.

We can expect the number of Hispanic Americans to continue to grow because many of them are young and, therefore, of child-bearing age, and because immigration from Latin America to the United States results in annual increases of over 100,000. Certain educational concerns are apparent from a 1976 HEW study *(Survey of Income and Education).* The study found that persons with Spanish language backgrounds in grades 5–12 were about twice as likely to be two or more grades below the grade level expected for their ages than were those with English-speaking backgrounds. Another finding from the study was that those with Spanish language backgrounds dropped out at a higher rate (45 percent) than the aggregate of other language minorities (30 percent).[4]

While Hispanic Americans will make up the largest group of non-English-speaking students, there will be many other students who can aptly be termed children of the "new immigrants." These new immigrants are primarily refugees. Approximately 14,000 refugees arrive in this country each month or about 200,000 a year, and most of these are from Indochina. While these refugees will not be found in all the schools over the nation, the numbers are fairly well dispersed in certain regions. It has been estimated by some demographers that immigration —legal and illegal—accounts for one-half of the present population growth in the United States. This fact has tremendous implications for schools of the 80's as they attempt to deal with students under court-mandated bilingual–bicultural programs. What happens if all groups want to maintain their ethnic identities? Further, how does an organization such as the school meet the needs of nonconformers to the system —in this case, these new immigrants are nonconformers in the sense that they have their own language and may be permitted to use it in the system for which conformity is to speak English?

Special treatment has been mandated for other groups of students such as the disadvantaged (under certain titles of ESEA) and groups of students who are being bused under court-ordered programs. Schools will continue to meet the mandates for special treatment for these groups of students as well as for those discussed above.

The second broad category of students who will receive special treatment in the schools of the 80's are those whose numbers will grow because of the pervasiveness of a particular problem and who are apt to attract a following that will demand that the schools mount campaigns or programs to deal with their needs.

An example of students falling into this category are those from the single-parent family. Concern for this group of students can be seen in the number of conferences already being held to deal with the question of single-parent families and what schools can do to meet needs of the youngsters who share this characteristic. There are over 6 million single-parent families today in our country, involving over 11 million children, most of them in school. In the last decade, the divorce rate doubled. In 1978 over 1 million marriages ended in divorce, affecting approximately 1 million children. Children affected by divorce are more likely to be in the 5- to 12-year-old age group than in any other.

The single-parent family is a viable unit with which the school must deal in the 80's. Current statistics from the U.S. Bureau of the Census, Marriage and Family Statistics Branch, show that approximately 67 percent of these single parents are separated or divorced; 13 percent are widowed; and 16 percent have never been married. Approximately 4 percent have been temporarily separated.[5] Between 1960 and 1970, single-parent families with children grew by 40 percent, while all families with children grew by 12 percent. Between 1970 and 1978, single-parent families grew by over 50 percent, while all families with children grew by only 5 percent. It is obvious that there has been a disproportionate growth in single-parent families. The proportion of children under 18 years of age living with one parent doubled between 1960 (9 percent) and 1978 (19 percent). The number of children living with never-married mothers jumped from 4 percent in 1970 to 14 percent in 1978.

Using 1960 as a base year, and projecting to 1990, the proportion of children under 18 years of age living with one parent at any given time will come close to tripling—from 9 percent in 1960 to 25 percent in 1990.[6] The sheer numbers of youngsters falling in this group, plus the obvious implication for schools, will virtually assure that this group of youngsters will receive special treatment in the 80's.

From studies already made in schools, the following conditions have been noted:[7]

1. School achievement drops off for a time for youngsters who experience the loss of a parent.

2. There is a need for counseling and stability.

3. The parent needs a different time frame for conferences; they may need help also.

4. In one survey, teachers noted that two-thirds of all youngsters showed some notable change in school following their parents' separation—the most notable in achievement.

5. For about one-half of these students, teachers reported a high level of anxiety; nearly one-fourth of the children had difficulty concentrating on school work.

6. Sadness or depression was noted in one-fifth of the students.

7. After one year most of the students appeared to have learned to cope.

Since the number of single-parent families is projected to increase, the youngsters from these families will be targeted to receive special treatment in the 80's.

Another group of students who will be targeted for special treatment in the 80's is comprised of those who face significant problems with which they need help. One need only to consider the statistics on drug abuse, alcohol abuse, unwanted pregnancy, suicide, violence, and unemployment to know something of the problems causing student stress. Whether these problems will be any more pronounced in the 80's than they were in the 70's remains to be seen—that the schools will be under pressure to help this varied group of students is a certainty.

There is, however, some reasonable doubt as to the efficacy of asking the schools to undertake this task in isolation from other social agencies. A very real need in the 80's will be to find ways to put youth into meaningful contact with adults other than those in education, adults who can guide adolescents in the maturation process. Young people are too much isolated from their elders in society. Perhaps if we planned for the transition from youth to adulthood and from the school world to the work world, we could reduce some of the stress on students. Until and unless we do, the schools will come under increasing pressure to deal with students facing the problems identified earlier.

Finally, I must refer to a group of students who do not fit into either of the previous categories—migrant children. Given the current economic conditions, this group may well increase in numbers. But they have no mandated programs, and they are not likely to have a vocal or organized group to press their cause. They are too often seen as statistics, not as real people. As a result, they are almost always ignored. We have been told of their plight over the years since the NEA produced the gripping documentary *A Desk for Billie* over 20 years ago. Migrants may be Black, White, Indian, Mexican American, or Puerto Rican. They are generally illiterate, poor, lacking the cultural background to fit into the dominant culture, and often in poor health. Because they follow work based on seasonal demands, they have no permanent residence. They are found along three routes: (1) the southeastern states from

Florida northward through the east coast states; (2) southern California, north through the Pacific coast states, and (3) the main stream, north and west from Texas to the north central, mountain, and Pacific coast states.

The children of the migrant workers could be the responsibility of schools in almost any of the states. The truth is, however, that they are generally no one's responsibility. Their educational experience lacks the continuity essential for academic growth. They rarely complete a school year, and nearly one-half never enter high school. They are a troublesome factor in neat, precise recordkeeping, and the school has a difficult time dealing with the deviancy from traditional prototypes that they represent.

Perhaps we can find ways of meeting the needs of this group of students who have, at best, suffered from benign neglect all these years. There are some faint glimmers of hope for these students. The routes of migration are known, and the students, once identified, could be looked for in certain schools at certain times during the year. A communication system might be established from one school to the next by which the educational experience of these students could be given some continuity. True, the migrants do not fit the bureaucratic prototype for the schools. But must this mean that they will continue to be ignored in the educational process?

I have suggested categories of students that the schools will be required to serve in the 80's. The typology from the Carnegie Report[8] was suggested as a productive approach to student classification. Identifying groups of students and then developing prototype programs for them is not new. The school does what any complex organization must do: it deals in prototype programs for prototype students.

Certain questions can be raised about the process being used to identify targeted groups for special treatment. Is the practice of mandating treatment through the courts or legislative bodies the most appropriate way of dealing with the educational needs of students? The handwriting is on the wall; if the school does not design programs for students with special needs, the courts and legislatures will. A second question is this: How many prototype programs can the school effectively implement simultaneously?

The problem is not with prototypes as such because we accept that this is a way of life for a complex organization; it is, rather, how we arrive at the prototypes we implement. Do we begin with a model of treatment, or do we begin with the client (the student) and design the model of treatment?

The tendency of any organization when prototypes are mandated from outside the organization, or even when they are generated from inside based on generalized truths, is to tighten up on the individuals delivering the service. In terms of the school this means maintaining the idealized prototype program and controlling the teacher who delivers the service.

A more desirable approach would be to loosen the constraints on the professional person delivering the service. The paradox, which is difficult for the bureaucratic organization to accept, is that the more the organization loosens up on the professional (the teacher) delivering the service, the more likely it is that the professional can accommodate the mandated prototypes, while at the same time meeting individual needs by developing prototypes based on specific student needs.

The teacher in the one-room school managed to do just that. No matter what idealized prototype the teacher brought to the job, it did not take long for that teacher to realize that she/he had to adapt that prototype to the characteristics of the students in that one room! Teachers in the schools of the 80's must have the same freedom to design flexible, imaginative, individual learning environments.

REFERENCES

1. The Carnegie Council on Policy Studies in Higher Education. *Giving Youth a Better Chance: Options for Education, Work, and Service.* Berkeley, Calif.: The Carnegie Foundation for the Advancement of Teachers, 1979. pp. 17–18.

2. Roybal, Edward R. "Hispanics: A Political Perspective." *Social Education* 43: 103; February 1979.

3. *Ibid.*

4. *Ibid.* p. 102.

5. Norton, Arthur J. "A Portrait of the One Parent Family." *The National Elementary Principal* 59: 34; October 1979.

6. *Ibid.* pp. 32–35.

7. Kelly, Joan B., and Wallerstein, Judith S. "Children of Divorce." *The National Elementary Principal* 59: 51–58; October 1979.

8. The Carnegie Council on Policy Studies in Higher Education. *Giving Youth a Better Chance.*

CHAPTER 4

Teacher Education for the 80's
Cordell Affeldt

Establishing teaching as a true profession is not simply a desirable development; it is a necessary one. We must enhance the status of teaching as a career in order to attract and hold creative, competent, dedicated personnel.

Teachers are faced with critical, recurring problems, and have little or no certainty that they can solve them. What teachers are taught in preservice programs and what they are asked to do in a classroom seem to have, on the surface, little relationship one to the other.

Although pressures will continue, and possibly increase, in the 80's to require teachers to perform as technicians, teacher education must raise the sights of teachers, permitting them to view teaching as more than a technical art. Teacher education must, of course, supply some basic survival skills; however, it must provide, in addition, a broad theoretical and philosophical base to allow teachers to do much more. Teacher education must focus more on educating a person who teaches than on training a teacher.

In this essay we will examine what teacher education should be in the 80's. Four components of teacher education will be discussed, as will the learning and teaching settings required. These components are self-knowledge, general knowledge, instructional knowledge, and professional knowledge.

Those predispositions and assumptions that have shaped the teacher's personal understanding of the world constitute the focus of *self-knowledge*. Achieving such self-understanding calls for recognizing hidden values. It encourages poking into one's personal history and examining societal, religious, familial, and educational experiences with a freshly observing eye. It demands uncovering prejudices, positive as well as negative. The purpose of the search for self-knowledge is to recognize the role that one's own personality plays in the teaching process.

Self-knowledge includes understanding how the teacher-to-be was taught. What was assumed about knowing? About learning? About teaching? What did the teachers of this future teacher assume? Many people who enter teaching do so as a confirmation of an earlier experience. They liked school, and, as a result, their own schooling easily becomes the guide by which they formulate their eventual teaching style. One teaching mode dominates. Because a teacher tends to teach in the way in which he or she was taught, receptivity to alternative approaches is stifled without the teacher's realizing that it has happened.

An emphasis on self-knowledge presumes the value of knowing what forces have shaped one's life. It does not presume greater value for some forces than for others. It militates against reflexive conservatism and favors diversity. It makes the teacher more receptive to accepting others from differing backgrounds. As an example, recognizing the relationship between culture and personal behavior is the first step a teacher can make toward relating successfully to the student from the single-parent home, the poor but academically talented student, the student from a non-English-speaking home. The prejudice of parochialism must be allowed to atrophy. Self-knowledge is a means for dealing with the veiled persuaders of the past and a facilitator for harmonizing interpersonal and intergroup dynamics.

In teacher education, knowledge of self is achieved primarily through process-oriented activities rather than through product-oriented activities. Talking time should be provided, and simulated and on-site experiences, as opposed to traditional, campus-based experiences, should be structured as a means of testing self in new situations.

The component of *general knowledge* could be equated with traditional general education or liberal studies. This focus must precede the study of teaching per se because teaching requires knowing *what* to teach as well as *how* to teach. Teachers must acquire sufficient expertise in the content of instruction to lead, guide, and otherwise assist learners.

Teachers of the future will work in a multicultural, often bilingual, student world. General knowledge should include a broad foundation in literature, history, anthropology, and philosophy. An intercultural view should be encouraged by including Eastern as well as Western cultures. World history should be just that—*world* history. World literature should be *world* literature.

A solid theoretical base should be provided in science, psychology, and sociology. Concepts and generalizations from a discipline, rather than a maze of disparate facts and specifics, should be learned. Getting at the theoretical base of a discipline reveals its broad principles. However, theoretical understanding should be pragmatically directed because theory undergirds the teacher's ability to evaluate instructional strategies. Such an understanding strengthens the teacher's capacity to tie together instructional theory and instructional practice.

Some will say that teacher training is far too theoretical now. It would be more correct to say that theory has been divorced from practice and that both have suffered in the process. Methods courses have tried to grow "how-to" under glass. The business of fertilizing and weeding in the real-life world of students has been fenced off from attention. The result has been to produce technicians of limited capacity instead of practiced professionals.

Teacher education has to do more than produce technicians. We anticipate a changing world for children; hence, teachers must be competent to deal with futures education. Gifted and talented students and academically and physically handicapped students will have increasingly complex learning expectations. Teacher education in the 80's must prepare teachers to understand the nature of knowledge and to utilize alternative ways of knowing.

In meeting the particular needs of students, teachers must diagnose cognitive status and behavioral syndromes, and utilize those diagnoses in decision making. Teachers will be asked to give increased attention to the process of evaluation and to make reasonable applications of pedagogical research.

Finally, the general knowledge component of teacher education should include a heavy emphasis on writing. Bluntly put, writing down one's thoughts demands developing some thoughts. Structure, logic, and clarity are all held to the light. Writing essays, summaries, and research papers provides opportunities for analysis or presentation, an essential element in later curricular planning. Expressing one's thoughts in writing requires clear thinking. The ability to ferret out knowledge calls for judgment and efficiency as well as being comfortable in the use of a resource center.

Instructional knowledge, the sum of knowledge of how to teach, is the third component of teacher education. It calls for the persistent pursuit of the relationship between scientific reasoning and pedagogical practice. Reading about teaching will not be enough. Practicing teaching will not be enough. The two must be inextricably fused.

From the research, a body of knowledge about instruction must be articulated. Then the principles of teaching and learning so identified should be used in the instructional process. These "rules of practice" will prove their value by raising the predictability of outcome: "Given this set of conditions, this is what I can/cannot teach this student at this particular time."

This aspect of teacher training has not been given enough attention in the past. It has been difficult to identify a particular set of principles that should form the basis of instruction in teacher training institutions, and, even when identified, they do not seem to have been tied to teacher behaviors and decision making. The lack of a universally accepted body of knowledge about teaching reinforces our dependence on self. Our work setting usually keeps us further isolated from each other. Collegiality has been avoided as a thief of time. But unless we collaborate in the establishment of a specific professional culture, we will continue to flounder in response to the demands of society.

The focus of the instructional knowledge component should include diagnosis and evaluation and related recordkeeping. Documenting decisions about students based on evaluation of their development and performance will become increasingly important as public expectations for the schools grow. Learning to work with small computers is a must for teachers because individual educational programs will become a reality for students only if recordkeeping is kept manageable.

Developmental psychology should be included in the focus on the instructional knowledge component, as should group dynamics. Economics demand that children continue to be dealt with in groups. Teachers can be effective only when they understand how groups function, what factors can affect their functioning, and what impact the teacher can have on group functioning.

This component of teacher education should give increased attention to speaking skills. Fluency, clarity, and adaptability should all be taught, as should elements of drama.

Extensive field experience, exposing teachers-to-be to exemplary teaching, is necessary. School-based teachers should be adjunct faculty of the teacher education institution from which the school accepts practicing teachers. The site-based education of the teachers-to-be should be as academically rigorous as the campus-based activities. Analysis and defense of instructional choices should be required practices. Routine, tactical, and strategic problem solving should not be left to chance. The links between theory and practice should be systematically forged.

Future teachers must develop the skills necessary (1) to formulate realistic, individualized developmental objectives; (2) to create, select, and organize learning experiences; (3) to select appropriate instructional materials; and (4) to define the space, time, and human requirements of the class activities chosen.

The fourth and final component, *professional knowledge*, should focus on relating instructional activities to the larger society. The social and political forces that have shaped American education should be examined. Traditionally this material has been given a once-over-lightly in Introduction to Education or saved for those who take administration courses. But in the 80's teachers, as well as administrators, must consider questions such as the following: How is education financed? Has the method of financing changed? If it has, why? Or if it hasn't, why not? Who determines curricular content? Who really selects materials? Who becomes an educator? Who does not? What role do teacher organizations play in shaping education? Teachers must also have a working knowledge of school law, particularly as it applies to students' rights, teachers' rights, and parents' rights. Teachers need to recognize the institutional constraints and expectations that are the backdrop against which instructional decisions are played out.

Professional knowledge refers also to what teachers know about the history of teaching as an occupation. The revolution of professionalization in teaching can best be understood by examining its history of semiprofessionalism. Self-selection has traditionally been the prime requisite for becoming a teacher. Society, acting through state governments, has offset the limited incentives of teaching by making access easy. Low-cost, dispersed, egalitarian training institutions have been created and nurtured. Tax funds have been more readily available to train teachers than to pay them higher salaries.

Teaching has carried a greater subjective penalty for men than it has for women. When compared to the traditional female alternatives —secretary or nurse—the pay was acceptable, and women were able to keep teaching in addition to focusing on their own families. Therefore, psychic rewards were accepted instead of money. For males, teaching was a route to greater economic security and higher social status than that of their parents. Teaching was institutionalized as temporary employment for men and as continuing employment for women.

Our current work circumstances attract and hold many persons who liked school as they found it, reinforcing a tendency to limited interest in instructional reform. Our academic preparation has brought little sense of shared trial. The course of study has not been notably demanding. Learn by doing. Take your trial by fire. If you get through the first year, you will probably be a successful teacher. The folk wisdom has told us that good teachers are born, not made.

Professional pride, a sense of guild, is built more through the process of teacher education than through its content. Study groups, team teaching, and high academic standards are all means to the end. Leadership training should receive increased attention in the 80's.

Converting teacher *training* to teacher *education* is a big order; such education cannot be provided in four years. A distinctive teaching degree, comparable to the L.L.B. or the M.D., should be established. The professional schools offering such a degree should function in tandem with community school systems, using the social influence of the work place as a resource instead of avoiding it as a problem. In order to enter these professional schools, students would be required to hold a Bachelor of Arts degree and pass a highly selective entrance examination.

Such a rigorous approach to teacher education will doubtless significantly reduce the number of available teachers. Clerical and instructional aides will be needed to assist teachers in reaching the many children for whose instruction they will be responsible. Teachers should constitute the curricular council of each school facility; instructing and offering instructional leadership are primary responsibilities of teachers.

The instruction of teachers should begin with self-knowledge, move to general knowledge, then to instructional knowledge, and finally to professional knowledge: Who am I, and why do I want to teach? What is the scope of what is known and knowable about the world in which my students will be growing up? How do I teach my students to live in that world? What are the forces shaping the educational system in which I will be working? This instruction should be provided by teacher education programs offered in site-based professional schools to students who have completed a Bachelor of Arts degree and passed an entrance examination.

Teacher education is at a critical point. We have the knowledge and experience to reform it. If teacher education is to make a difference in education in the 80's, we need to begin the task of restructuring the programs for preparing teachers to the end that we are educating a person who teaches rather than simply training a teacher.

CHAPTER 5

The Teacher and the Taught: Declining Student Populations and the Effects of That Decline on Schools, Teaching, and the School Program

Margaret Gill Hein

"Declining," "shrinking," "belt-tightening," and "less" are words that are bringing anxiety and trauma into the hearts of educators who are engaged in an enterprise that for several decades has been described as "growing," "expanding," and "more." The drastic change indicated by comparison of these two sets of adjectives confronts educators with a climate of constraint and suggests necessary but painful reductions in resources: students and dollars.

Retrenchment lurks. Restrictions are inevitable. Either of these conjures up visions of personal limitations for teachers and administrators, and eventually for students unless bold and prompt actions are taken. These visions of restriction and limitation spread quickly to the learning climate, which is the total school environment.

The outlook is somber when extrapolated from the discouraging fact alone that the birth rate in the United States reached a peak of 4.3 million in 1961 and then continued to decline steadily until it leveled at about 3.2 million in 1973. This fact and the resultant apprehensive, negative feelings are converging at the very time when critics of the schools have already slowed innovative programs because education reforms have not lived up to the critics' expectations; in their view, society's problems remain unsolved and, in fact, unimproved.

Illustrative of this outlook is the fact that in 1980, for the first time, the American Association of School Administrators (AASA) listed public confidence on its questionnaire regarding big problems. Public confidence was named a major problem by 52 percent of the respondents.[1] Such a response heightens the concern for the negatives because the views people hold do help to shape the future and can become self-justifying; and, if they are not self-justifying, they at least reinforce an innate desire for survival, a need for security, and, thus, a move to maintain the status quo.

There is no way to predict the future accurately, regardless of futurists' claims. Even now when the student population is generally declining, some geographical areas of the South and the Southwest are experiencing just the opposite—growth. Education's history is shaped just as much by intangibles, good or bad, as by hard facts. There is no way to predict how the events of history, of which education is a part, will converge. No one can predict the working of the human mind, which will soon be revealed most vividly and forcefully in the persons and actions of the current education leaders. Factors external to the schools—as well as the internal factor now being considered, the number of students—do not require a decline in dynamism and quality. What happens will be a matter of deliberate choice—the working of human minds.

Education leaders are faced with a major decision: how to confront decline. Two options—one negative, the other imaginative—are available. The *negative* leader will act as she/he did in the past when confronted with growth, by simply responding to the conditions of the times; this type of leader was concentrating on building buildings and hiring bodies for classrooms. Faced with the present opposite situation, this individual will simply focus on current conditions—i.e., reduced budgets, shrinking enrollments, and closing schools. In other words, this type of leader will administer the routine; she or he will manage survival, avoid disaster, drift, muddle through, remain timid and react as demands surface, and possibly make overeager promises.

By contrast, the *imaginative* leader will assume vigorous academic leadership and will not compromise academic integrity. This leader will cope aggressively, will make bold moves, and will not preside over the dismantling of a school system. She/he knows that plans must be made for a different future to meet the twenty-first century. She/he will seize the opportunity to make *less* better, to improve elementary and secondary schooling. Stated simply, the imaginative leader will *plan to cope,* which means to work with her or his colleagues to find reasonable solutions to whatever problems lie ahead. Energies will be turned toward guaranteeing the high quality of schooling that has long been talked about but too little demonstrated. Planning becomes crucial. It may be too late for some school districts and some states to undertake the long-range planning that has been done, for example, by New York and Minnesota; but lack of time is no excuse not to begin planning as far in advance as possible.

DECISION: Plan to Cope

Find Reasonable Solutions to Problems

Cope with what? There will still be births, periods for these children to grow and develop, and someone to direct that development. Schools are not going to change the number of potential students; all those who will be in high school in the 1980's are already born. There will be

- Students, regardless of number
- Teaching and learning.
- Programs, something to be learned.

STUDENTS, REGARDLESS OF NUMBER

Some are calling the expected enrollment decline a golden age for students who now can truly be the center of attention and can expect to be taught and advised very conscientiously. Students can be looked at and listened to as individuals with unique learning styles and needs. During the years in which the educational system was growing, teachers confronted with increasing numbers of students deplored the lack of time to concentrate on the individual learner. Given fewer students at all levels, the quality of life in school can be analyzed, not deplored, and, one can hope, improved.

In the first reports from "A Study of Schooling," directed by John Goodlad over a six-year period, several observations about student life in schools are made. Observations of data collectors and experiences recorded by students suggest that as the level of schooling increases, the academic self-concepts of students show a slight decline.[2] This perception of differences suggests that perhaps the actual experiences of students as they interact with teachers do indeed differ from elementary to secondary schools. Why? What are the implications for enhancing academic self-concepts during this period of declining enrollments?

In one high school referred to in the study, students agreed that "too many students at this school are allowed to graduate without learning very much."[3] If a given faculty, taking a similar look at what is happening to its students, should find a comparable reaction, what steps should it take to improve schooling for the students? The idea is for each student to find school worthwhile for her or him.

During a 1979 survey high school students in eight counties of North Carolina were asked to choose from a list of problems those that they considered most serious in their schools. The results were compared with those of the 1977 and 1978 Gallup polls. The Gallup polls most consistently mentioned "lack of discipline," but students in the North Carolina schools surveyed identified "pupils who just don't care."[4] Does this difference suggest that students are the most accurate in identifying problems in their schools? Does this also suggest that students should be involved in identifying the problems in order that they can subsequently be involved in solving the problems, and, thus, learn the skills of problem solving? Any number of studies of school-age groups reveal that students do not see themselves as involved in meaningful decisions about their life in schools. How can students be involved in coping with the problems of declining enrollments?

The literature has long documented the fact that the young are kept segregated as age groups: elementary, middle school or junior high, and senior high. The apparent basis for this segregation is tradition, rather than knowledge about students. For example, educators concerned with middle schools admit there are no agreed-upon, optimal age limits for the in-between group.

When there are fewer K–12 students, energies should be directed to whatever sources of students are available outside the customary age groups. Why not open schools to all ages? There is no evidence that a 10-year-old cannot learn Chinese, for example, with a 16-year-old; or that either or both of them cannot learn Chinese with a 60-year-old.

The school-age population has been kept apart from the outside world. Why can't interested adults enroll in high school or junior high school classes? Adults are volunteering to be aides, tutors, and guest lecturers, and to fill other teaching roles. Why not allow them to enroll in classes and assume the learner role where appropriate? Educators must examine age as now used as a major criterion for grouping learners.

In Harbor Springs, Michigan, the secondary school library has been turned into a center for senior citizens who will also have the use of all the school facilities; they can mingle with students as teacher aides, guest speakers, or tutors, and enroll in classes. The teachers had in-service training on the aging, and the students had two weeks of study of aging, new content in their classes. Bob Doan, project director, said, "We just can't afford the luxury of single-use facilities anymore. And these people have spent a life-time paying taxes."[5]

New information about the aging, new skills, and new relation-ships resulting from a new mix of ages in the schools can lead to an imaginative way of coping with the needs of a community and its schools when space becomes available.

TEACHING AND LEARNING

As school staffs become older, their higher salaries make them more expensive; and the public sees them as more conservative and less resilient, less able to adjust to the present. Even if the public's percep-tion is incorrect, the teachers and administrators are farther removed from the age of their students, and they can be less dynamic, less enthusiastic, less motivated. Given current tenure and retirement poli-cies, even a stable community can bring in few new, young, enthusiastic teachers with vitality and fresh outlooks, not to mention fresh ideas about teaching and teaching techniques. Without the addition of new blood, a faculty situation will often deteriorate. If retrenchment does become a reality, the new and the young faculty members will be hardest hit; and some of the most promising prospective teachers will be denied the opportunity even to begin a teaching career.

The AASA poll mentioned above listed school financing as the first major problem, followed by cost reduction; however, 52 percent of the respondents named as a major problem the dismissal of incompetent staff.[6] Some faculty members may lose their jobs; but as the situation now exists, retrenchment will not be used to eliminate the weak. Teacher organizations will focus on security and strict adherence to seniority in dismissal cases, replacing their past focus on pay increases. Losses in real income can be expected for educators.

An additional restraint surfaces when there are few chances for teachers to advance into consultant and administrative jobs. There will be fewer of these jobs; some of these positions will be eliminated by attrition and retirement, and the people who fill the remaining positions are likely to stay put. As opportunities for advancement lessen, stagna-tion sets in, accompanied by dissatisfaction and personal animosities. Here are the ingredients for a negative environment.

Imaginative leaders can arrange to retrain staff as needs arise, to reassign or redeploy, and to reallocate faculty time in exciting ways to accommodate strengths or to readjust for lack of depth in some subject matter areas. Adjacent school districts can share faculty if the number of students in each does not justify a full-time teacher for some particular subject. These staffing changes offer promises of what can be done in an otherwise dismal situation.

The situation will not be dismal if teachers seize the initiative to build on their strengths and to insist on maintaining, or in some cases setting, high standards for faculty performance. Teachers must demonstrate that they are capable of developing and maintaining the highest quality of teaching, and, furthermore, that they can continue to improve their teaching skills, regardless of their ages and years spent in teaching, and regardless of the change in the number of students to be taught. How? By concentrating on improving instruction. How? By the study of teaching as a separate field of study such as educational psychology or educational sociology.

DECISION: To Study Teaching

A large body of literature on teaching exists, but it is largely ignored in the lives of teachers. Once they leave campus classes where initial entry-level certification is obtained, few teachers devote time to teaching as a field of study. In pre-service teacher education programs, method courses are the chief offerings dealing with teaching; in these courses emphasis for the most part is on specific techniques and procedures. The novice cannot be expected to analyze and adjust to all the variables interacting and converging at a given time in a given class because she/he is too preoccupied, and rightly so, with each day's plans, preparations, and paper-grading.

Professional meetings and in-service days offer opportunities for teachers who are seeking new techniques or new materials to take back to their classroom to meet their immediate needs. Even though the exchanges among peers at the increasingly popular Teacher Centers are valuable, these do not constitute a deliberate, systematic, intensive study of teaching.

How many teachers are familiar with the first *Handbook of Research on Teaching* (N.L. Gage, editor) published in 1963? Or the *Second Handbook of Research on Teaching* (M.W. Travers, editor) published in 1973? The same question can be asked about *The Language of the Classroom* (Arno Bellack and others) published in 1966, or *Ways of Teaching* (Ronald T. Hyman), the first edition of which was published in 1970 and the second in 1974, or *The Evaluation of Teaching*, which Pi Lambda Theta published in 1967. These randomly mentioned titles suggest a type of literature that can offer support for any teacher engaged in the daily direction of learning or in a regularized study of teaching. It is highly probable that such books as these have been used only in graduate courses, if indeed they have been used at all.

Any faculty serious about improving teaching should consider the benefits to be derived from organizing a course or a series of seminars for the consideration of teaching as a valid field of study, a field of study that promises immediate results in the form of new understandings and new ways of analyzing interactions in the classroom or, stated another way, promises improvement of teaching. Someone will mention the time required for such study and state that teachers are busy. Teachers are human; teachers are individuals. Those who want to improve their skills will soon recognize that time devoted to self-examination and self-study of one's teaching will bring positive results. When the schools were growing, such study was desirable; now such efforts could determine a teacher's survival in a restrictive climate.

How many teachers videotape to analyze their teaching? The necessary equipment is now easy to operate and inexpensive; yet, its use, however valuable, is hardly to be expected when one recalls the audio-visual vs. curriculum or the machine vs. instruction debates that far too long dissipated educators' energies. In fact, with the exception of the copying machine which requires little preparation and offers instant results, teachers do little with the vast array of instructional equipment and materials readily available and advocated in all curriculum literature for decades.

One report of lack of use can be cited from the Goodlad study referred to earlier. Student responses and observer reports agree that in English classes, media and materials associated with innovative teaching (such as films, tapes, slides, simulations, and records) receive minimal use. These materials were reported as *not* used by more than half of the students sampled in 13 high schools.[7] This is only one recent example; the literature has been filled with the same type of examples in other subjects since the days of teaching machines. Teachers may need to reexamine why such a very long road runs *from* availability of these instructional tools and the literature urging their use *to* their classrooms.

At some point between elementary school and senior high school, there is a shift in teachers' supportive behavior. Elementary teachers have been accused of overdoing praise to the point that some students and observers consider adjectives of praise such as "wonderful" and "good" and a nod of the head to be automatic responses and not evaluative. Less teacher encouragement of students continues to be found by observers of secondary classes. Can there be a significant relationship between this kind of teacher behavior and the declining academic self-concept as years of schooling increase? How does the perceived lack of support contribute to the feeling of some high school students that school is not a place where they are experiencing a good education? Examining this one aspect of teacher behavior does not require large expenditures of money or outside help; a tape recorder or a videotaping machine will easily suffice, leaving the teacher free to examine her/his words and gestures when convenient. As a group, teachers could examine their supportive behavior, or lack of it, and decide how this one variable influences life in their classrooms.

Recent surveys of how students are learning science are discouraging. The National Research Council (NRC) has found that curriculums using inquiry methods which were developed with federal funds in the 1950's and 1960's are little used; students learning science now listen, read, and memorize. NRC has also found that many new teachers do not know that the inquiry-based materials exist, even though the "concept" courses are now available in textbooks. Even if teachers are trained to use the inquiry approach, the current educational climate does not favor learning by exploration; emphasis on accountability and competency testing favors simple objectives rather than the learning of concepts and relationships.[8] However, the AASA list of major problems shows that accountability, which was 8th in major problems in 1974–75, was 52nd in 1980, a drastic fall from prominence. Unfortunately, the critics' influences are converging!

PROGRAMS, SOMETHING TO BE LEARNED

There is a need to document clearly the essentials that teachers are supposed to teach. The states' mandates should be examined thoroughly to make sure that current lists of requirements are correct. Documenting essentials does not have to lead to a "back to the 3 R's" argument if teachers and administrators seize the lead in explaining clearly what it is that they are trying to accomplish and why. Fads come and go regularly. We have vacillated from emphasis on liberal arts to vocational to career education, with the affective and the humane moving in and out with these swings. At present there is no common, comprehensive, widely accepted statement of goals of education.

In attempts to placate societal demands whenever they surface, educators have at times ignored their own best knowledge, judgment, and professional convictions about what *general education should be.* In exchange they have been charged with stifling the intellectual and with graduating students who cannot read or spell.

In attempting to react to society's problems, the schools have taken on too much. School personnel do not have the training, the skills, or the time to take care of such serious problems as economic deprivation, family instability, drug rehabilitation, or serious emotional disturbances. Other institutions in society are better equipped, and even have mandates, to work in these problem areas. A period of restriction must not be viewed as an opportunity to overload the schools with responsibility for the solution of these and other similar problems. The schools must admit that they have taken on too much and have promised results that never were attainable. This time of declining enrollments may be the opportune time to speak out against expectations for school services that are not clearly instructional because taxpayers are also in a limiting, restrictive mood and are not likely to finance enterprises that they see as inappropriate. If educators remain sensitive to the changes that are required to meet diverse student needs, and if they adhere to providing the essentials to meet these needs, the schools can do well what only the schools know how to do.

Data from "A Study of Schooling" show that teachers appear to be fairly well satisfied with the curriculum and what they do with it; they appear satisfied with their choices of content and teaching techniques, and are little influenced by state or district guidelines or consultants. Teachers see themselves in control of their teaching and are satisfied with it. Students make few decisions about their school work, and their parents are not involved in curriculum decisions.[9]

Given the fact that teachers do make most of the classroom-level decisions, should a way be found to facilitate communication among all who share responsibility with the teachers for the school experiences of children and youth? Should administrators, consultants, and counselors who have such responsibility be involved in any curriculum decisions? How might parents' opinions enhance these decisions? Opening lines of communication could foster improvement of teaching and provide an avenue to publicize the high standards held by teachers.

The prospect of small classes should lighten the hearts of teachers who have long been burdened with overly large classes. However, small classes can be viewed as a luxury for high-salaried teachers with too-small workloads. Advanced classes at the high school level, already small, must not suffer. Small classes can certainly be justified. The literature has been calling for individualized instruction to a far greater extent than teachers have been providing it. Teachers can now tailor the curriculum to the needs of individual learners. Time will be available to plan, to devise learning activities and instructional materials, and to advise students. The results obtained when teachers work with small groups and with individual students offer strong evidence of the value of time spent in individualizing instruction.

Elementary teachers individualize more frequently than do teachers in junior high school, and junior high school teachers have more ways of individualizing than do secondary teachers. Nongraded, multiage grouping and continuous progress have been frequently used in elementary schools; ability grouping, tracking, and advance placement have been used in high schools.

Grouping is the most common form of individualization. Teachers use their own judgment more than test scores in making decisions regarding classroom grouping and individualization. Veteran teachers were not taught the skills of individualizing and may not have developed their own. Although recommendations to individualize exceed practice, the prospect of fewer students may encourage teachers to try individualizing, which is not in reality a new teaching tool, but will be a new tool for some.

The specialized and technical services required for teaching may be provided by the state or by a county or regional office. When new bodies of knowledge become available in which teachers have not been trained, public education and higher education can work together in arranging necessary courses; in fact, there are untapped areas of instruction in which the two levels of education can work together.

DECISION: To Provide Essentials for Learning

NEGATIVE VS. IMAGINATIVE

Whole-hearted and whole-minded commitment from all educators is essential. Also mandatory is a relationship between a principal and her/his teachers that is more professional than American education has known in the past. One hopes that the principal has been the instructional leader. In case she/he has not been perceived as that, she/he must become the leader. The principal knows the total school best. The principal must have instructional leadership skills. If these skills are lacking, either the principal must be retrained, just as a teacher may need to be retrained, or someone with the requisite skills must be put into the position. Each school staff must be guided by the competence and convictions of a creative, *imaginative* leader.

Attention may be given to organizational structures that influence the learning environment and the curriculum. With the coming of the computer, changing time and calendar structures is not difficult. The difficulty will be in convincing adults of the desirability of different working hours. Flexible scheduling of whatever arrangement desired can accommodate work/study students; for example, early morning, late afternoon, and early evening classes can be scheduled for students who hold regular jobs. Year-round schools which nobody ever really wanted can be put into operation if a community can benefit from that organization of the school year. Consortia of schools within a district or of districts can share resources: teachers, students, facilities, or instructional materials. These arrangements, and many, many others yet to be thought of can contribute to making *less* better.

Never overlook the fact that organizational arrangements will not solve curriculum and instructional problems; coping with life in classrooms will. If teachers learn to cope with children and youth as these children and youth are learning to cope with their daily problems, both groups will be prepared to face an uncertain future. Daily interactions in classrooms are the major impact of schooling for students and teachers.

Maybe the creativity of educators was dulled by the comfort of "more," "growing," "expanding." Maybe ingenuity was dulled by the complacency of size. It does not follow, however, that a school system must be dismantled because of a new and drastically different situation —i.e., fewer students and fewer dollars. Pay attention to the writers, and to one's own convictions, that say, "Seize the opportunity to improve the quality of life in schools: to set very high standards for professional commitment and for professional performance." There will continue to be *some students* who will receive *some kind of teaching,* and there will be *something to be learned.*

Among the animals on the earth, it has been said, that only mankind can dream. Other species laugh, cry, love, rage, kill. Humans alone have the power to imagine tomorrow. Educators can envision tomorrow. Educators can cope; they can find imaginative, reasonable solutions to the problems arising from a declining student population. They can imagine tomorrow.

REFERENCES

1. Education USA. "Public Confidence Joins AASA List of Big Problems." *Education USA* 27(22): 202; March 3, 1980.

2. Benham, Barbara J.; Giesen, Phil; and Oakes, Jeannie. "A Study of Schooling: Students' Experiences in Schools." *Kappan* 61(5): 338; January 1980.

3. *Ibid.*

4. Pittman, Robert B., and Cloud, Lewis E. "Major Problems in Public Education from the Students' Perspective." *Kappan* 61(6): 425; February 1980.

5. Education USA. "Michigan School Adds Senior Citizen Center." *Education USA* 22(26): 194; February 25, 1980.

6. Education USA. "Public Confidence Joins AASA List of Big Problems."

7. Benham, Barbara J.; Giesen, Phil; and Oakes, Jeanne. *op. cit.* pp. 338–339.

8. Phi Delta Kappan. "Inquiry-Based Science Studies Are Giving Way to Rote Learning, NRC Says." *Phi Delta Kappan* 61(3): 225; November 1979.

9. Klein, M. Frances; Tye, Kenneth A.; and Wright, Joyce E. "A Study of Schooling: Curriculum." *Phi Delta Kappan* 61(4): 246–247; December 1979.

CHAPTER 6

Teacher Stress and Burnout
Willard H. McGuire

"To be burned out you once had to be on fire."

Thousands of sensitive, thoughtful, and dedicated teachers are leaving their profession because of *burnout*. [1] Burnout—caused by stress —threatens to reach epidemic proportions if it is not checked soon.

Hans Selye, identified by many as the father of stress research, defines *stress* as the "nonspecific response of the body to any demand made on it." [2] When a stressful event occurs, the body rallies to protect itself from the effects of stress and to adjust to the demand. It does this by producing chemicals in an effort to maintain bodily health and stability—and this works under most conditions. When the demands are excessive, however, the body exhausts its resources, adjustments are more difficult to make, and burnout occurs.

Alfred M. Bloch, assistant clinical professor at the University of California, Los Angeles, describes teachers' stress symptoms as similar to those of "people who have suffered from combat neurosis" and of "survivors of war disasters." [3] In short, they appear to have combat fatigue. Others have described teachers' stress symptoms as similar to those of upper-level executives and police.

Is teacher stress and burnout a national problem? A few facts about events that cause teacher stress:

62

- In 1974, 23 percent of college students said that they wanted to teach after graduation. In 1979, only 13 percent gave teaching as their occupational goal.

- The number of assaults on teachers increased from 70,000 in 1977–78 to over 110,000 in 1978–79—an increase of more than 50 percent in one year!

- In 1978–79, one-fourth of the nation's 2.1 million teachers suffered damage to or loss of personal property.

- Job security was once a positive consideration for those who chose teaching as their life profession. Now thousands of teachers are without jobs and thousands more are threatened with layoffs.

- During 1978–79, American school children committed 100 murders, 12,000 armed robberies, 9,000 rapes, and thousands of aggravated assaults against teachers and others. They were responsible for 270,000 burglaries and vandalism estimated to cost taxpayers more than $600 million yearly.[4]

The 1979 NEA Representative Assembly considered the situation so serious that it adopted the following resolution on teacher stress:

> The National Education Association believes that the dynamics of our society and increased public demands on education have produced adverse and stressful classroom and school conditions. These conditions have led to increased emotional and physical disabilities among teachers and other school personnel.
>
> The Association urges its local affiliates, in cooperation with local school authorities, to develop stress management programs that will facilitate the recognition, prevention, and treatment of stress-related problems.
>
> The Association further urges that the harmful effects of stress on teachers and other school personnel be recognized, and it demands procedures that will ensure confidentiality and treatment without personal jeopardy.

What is it in teachers' lives that causes them to be susceptible to stress as defined by Professor Selye? Is it a new phenomenon in the teaching profession? Are there alterations that can be made in the way schools are run that can ameliorate teacher stress? Where can and should those alterations be made?[5]

THREE CAUSES OF STRESS

There are, doubtless, hundreds of reasons why teacher stress is so much with us today. For one thing, we live in a world that is more anxious than ever before about its future. The nature of knowledge and the nature of those who are to be taught have changed, and adults with responsibilities for youth are unclear about how to help them.

Three problem areas are worth exploring because improvements in these areas could do much to alleviate some root problems that contribute to teacher stress.

The Teacher's Preprofessional Education

Recently 800 Oklahoma teachers were asked if their collegiate preparation provided the skills and information necessary to meet the challenges they found in the schools. Not one hand was raised in that large audience; not one teacher's voice affirmed being properly trained for work in the classroom. Imagine the stress when a teacher discovers the difference between the expectations that result from college preparation and the on-the-job realities.

The almost two and one-half million teachers currently in U.S. classrooms have a combined personal investment in their baccalaureate education of more than $100 billion. Teacher training institutions are as underfunded and as unduly criticized as are elementary and secondary schools. But it is tragic to consider that the billions of dollars teachers have paid out have provided for so little accountability from their preparation programs. Teachers have a right to professional education that relates to what will be expected of them.

At the same time there is a significant public outcry that teachers generally lack competence. What is the solution to this alleged condition? Amazingly, many think it is necessary to spend millions of dollars to verify candidates' readiness for certification using paper-and-pencil tests—tests that are racist in their effect, psychometrically incompetent, and inapplicable to the work the prospective teachers will do.

The answer does not lie in superficialities such as these tests. It lies in high-quality preparation programs: programs that are carefully and professionally conceived, carried out, and evaluated; programs that draw theory and practice into closer proximity; programs that are adequately financed and continually modified according to the experiences of their graduates out there in the real world of teaching. A well-prepared teacher experiences less stress.

The Reward System for Teachers

While the ethic of most teachers is that old maxim "Meet the needs of your students," the modus operandi of too many school systems is efficiency, positive public relations, and maintenance of the status quo. Thus, while a teacher—particularly a new one—seeks satisfaction in relationships with students, in growth particular to the individual student, and in the creation and maintenance of an exciting learning environment, the school system rewards other kinds of behavior: punctuality, high scores on standardized tests that often are unrelated to the real needs of students, and a quiet, businesslike atmosphere. This reward system is out of sync with the major purposes of schooling, and the result for many teachers, particularly those who care deeply about the quality of schooling, is stress.

To keep school today, teachers and principals are required to spend countless hours performing an extraordinary number of tasks unrelated in the long run to what youngsters need to be able to know and do. These range from supervising groups of students not engaged in their studies to completing all manner of forms. Teachers know, and research is now confirming, that the single most important factor in increased student achievement is *time-on-task*. Simply put, learning takes time. The more time students and teachers have to spend on the curriculum, the better the outcome. Teachers feel robbed when they are not permitted to be so engaged with their students—and the product is frustration that can end up as stress.

Teachers also feel out of step with certain student behaviors and with the response of legal authorities and some parents to those behaviors. It is true that some schools and communities have come up with creative solutions to help students who are not able to succeed in the regular classroom setting. Improved counseling services, "crisis rooms," parent involvement programs, and the like have helped these students to acquire the skills and attitudes necessary to participate in learning. These techniques also have helped free other students from the disturbing influences of the problem children. And they have made it possible for teachers to teach.

In too many schools, though, teachers have to spend inordinate amounts of time dealing with the small minority of uncooperative, disruptive students. In that setting, no one wins. Since the system blames teachers for unruly classrooms and rewards them for quiet ones, teachers' efforts will continue to attempt to reduce disruptive student behavior.

The conflict of role—policeperson/teacher—is a real producer of stress. Policing produces stress; teaching relieves stress.

Esteem for the Teacher

Teachers obviously live their personal lives in the same stressful society as nonteachers. However, they find themselves subject to a few differences.

They are, for instance, required to have a license or certificate, the purpose of which is to attest to the holder's teaching skill. The granting of the license is a political act, the state's official endorsement of the teacher's competence. Theoretically, the state has nobody to blame but itself when a license is inappropriately issued. But teachers find their profession being blamed for the alleged deficiencies.

How, then, should a teacher view public complaints by politicians and education managers and more demands for teacher accountability in areas controlled by nonteachers? All teachers should come to understand that politicians and editorialists who complain about the quality of education should complain to themselves because apparently inadequate practices continue unabated and unchanged.

There may be a small percentage of America's teachers who do not have a good grasp of their subject matter, and there are a few who do but still are not good teachers. The vast majority, though, are more than adequate. How discouraging, how stressful it is for them to be barraged by headlines and magazine covers that proclaim their incompetence!

TOWARD GREATER PRODUCTIVITY

It is clearly not in the best interest of students, parents, or the public school system to continue practices that are causing thousands of our teachers to experience job-related stress, burnout, and dropout. Schools need to become more satisfying places for teachers and learners. They need to be places in which teaching and learning are central, in which every action contributes to that central purpose. A number of steps toward a more desirable educational setting must be initiated.

Improve Teacher Education

As previously indicated, the nature of teacher preparation programs must be altered so that they more nearly reflect the world of practice and so that they teach the potential teacher how to thrive rationally in that setting. A small first step in that direction is for colleges of education to appoint advisory panels of classroom teachers. These panels can help to keep the faculty alert to conditions in the schools and to ensure that teacher education students are prepared to work in that world.

Consider Legislative Impact

Legislators' intent to do good by mandating more and more programs for teachers to implement must be tempered with concern for the context in which instruction must take place, for an already overloaded school program, and for the staff development necessary to give teachers the skills they need to do the implementing. Public leaders at every level—federal, state, and local—must be oriented to the roles of teachers and must make decisions based on the practicalities of the classroom.

Increase Teacher Decision Making

The classroom responsibilities of teachers should be coupled with a corresponding degree of control. Teachers must have more to say about what, how, when, and with what resources they will teach in order to better meet the needs of their individual students. As John Goodlad reminds us, the best educational decisions are made at the level closest to the learner.

Improve Administrative Support

School administrations must make new efforts to provide a more supportive and secure school environment so that teachers can expend their energies teaching and students can spend their time learning. Every administrative action should be directed toward this central purpose of schooling—helping teachers teach and students learn; helping create a reality of education rather than just an appearance of order.

Decrease School Violence

National, state, and local education and government leaders and the public must bring massive efforts to bear on the eradication of violence and vandalism in the schools. Adequate monetary and human resources can help to alleviate this major threat to teaching and learning. Drastic reductions in class size, for example, will allow for more individualized instruction and for more extensive teacher counseling of students. Parents and organized community groups must give their support if schools are to be safe places for students and teachers.

Raise the Priority of Education

Public education must be given the financial priority necessary to make the fullest use of the nation's educational resources. Present funding levels must be increased to provide for a teaching force large enough to eliminate overcrowded classrooms; to provide appropriate education for students with special needs; to encourage the gifts and talents of all students; to upgrade instructional materials; to allow teachers adequate preparation periods; and to offer teachers sabbaticals and other opportunities to reflect on their work.

Increase Public Awareness

The public must be given better information about teachers' work. The schools are providing a service vital to the continued growth of our nation. Unfortunately, the media all too often are not helping citizens to understand and make wise judgments about these schools. There is much that is good, interesting, and newsworthy in classrooms, and the press with its enormous skills could make a great contribution to the quality of life by seeking out those situations and telling the public about them.

Act on Short-Term Remedies

Educators, school board members, and district administrators must together plan and implement procedures that will either prevent teacher stress and burnout before they occur or deal with them if they do occur. A growing number of programs are available for teachers experiencing work-related stress. Enlightened employment practices that benefit teachers and the school system are in place now in a few districts. Those on both sides of the bargaining table need to be aware of these options and use them in their agreements.

Our students deserve and need competent teachers on fire with ideas, enthusiasm, and commitment. Too much of what goes on in schools is diminishing this passion. Those who care about the future lives of students should be concerned with improving the current lives of their teachers.

REFERENCES

1. Alschuler, Alfred S., et al., eds. *Teacher Burnout*. Washington, D.C.: National Education Association, 1980.

2. Selye, Hans. *Stress Without Distress*. New York: New American Library, 1974.

3. Bloch, Alfred M. "The Battered Teacher." *Today's Education* 66: 58–61; March/April 1977.

4. The statistics are drawn from NEA Research findings and from: Cronley, Connie. "Blackboard Jungle Updated." *TWA Ambassador*, September/October 1978.

5. Swick, Kevin J., and Hanley, Patricia E. *Stress and the Classroom Teacher*. Washington, D.C.: National Education Association, 1980.

Part III

THE SCHOOL PROGRAM: THE NATURE OF THE CURRICULUM FOR THE 80's

. . . in the 30's during the heyday of progressive education, the child was the primary focus. In the 40's, when we were engaged in a great world war, the curriculum was society-centered. In the 50's and 60's the scholars were in the saddle, and the curriculum was primarily subject- or discipline-centered. . . . in the 70's, we [were] concerned with the total curriculum for all children. Hopefully [in] the 80's we will have a truly humanistic curriculum.

Ask . . . your students about the sun. What will [they] tell you? It is 93,000,000 miles from the earth, approximately 866,500 miles in diameter, with a surface rotation of about 25 days at the equator. If [they are] to live in the shadow of bigger and better bombs, perhaps [they] must be taught all these facts. Yet, it will always be the larger purpose of education to lead [them] to appreciate the radiance of a sunset.

Ole Sand

CHAPTER 7

The School Program:
Curriculum and Teaching in the 80's

John I. Goodlad

In 1959, the National Education Association established the Project on the Instructional Program of the Public Schools and gave it a major task: Make thoughtful and creative recommendations to serve as a guide to the profession and the public in their combined efforts to study and improve the quality of the instructional program in the schools. Ole Sand wrote the following in the preface of the three basic volumes commissioned by the Project:

> The facts of our twentieth century life—a rapidly changing society, a mounting store of knowledge, and new understandings about people and about learning—create some basic problems relating to the instructional program of the schools. There is no shortage of ideas about what these problems are and how they should be solved. There is, in fact, a constant babble of voices as millions of people with many and often conflicting ideas speak out about education.[1]

The broad facts of twentieth century life remain, intensifying old problems and creating new ones. The babble of voices continues. And the need to find a guiding sense of direction for the schools is as great as or greater than it was two decades ago.

Several of the questions posed by the National Committee for the Project on Instruction, appointed to carry on the work of the Project, invite the development of a curriculum agenda for the 80's. One question in particular guides what follows: How can the instructional program of the schools be designed to develop the individual potentialities of all members of the school population within the framework of a society that values both unity and diversity? Unfortunately, this question has not been well attended to. It has not been the subject of sustained dialogue at any level of the educational system—and our schools now show the signs of curricular neglect.

OLD PROBLEMS IN NEW DRESS

If preliminary findings from a small sample of carefully selected schools in "A Study of Schooling"[2] are at all representative of more schools, then momentous curriculum development tasks beg for attention. I use here, first, a cluster of data pertaining to the 13 senior high schools in our sample and, later, data from the 25 elementary and junior high schools—schools diverse in size, socioeconomic status and ethnicity of students, rural/metropolitan location, and regional distribution.

Those developing the programs of the schools in our sample are apparently seeking to respond to diversity in their student populations. Curricular offerings are many and varied, appearing to be limited only by the size of teaching staffs. The curriculum Conant recommended in 1959 for the comprehensive high school is, by contrast, spare and lean.[3] But one is forced to wonder if a proliferation in courses is the best response to human individuality. The concept of unity appears to have been lost.

Our data suggest the dominance in these schools of two provisions for diversity. First, there appears to be an assumption that the school should assure, on one hand, the preparation of students for more advanced studies and the professions and, on the other, the preparation to go into jobs before or directly after high school graduation. Clearly, there were students emphasizing academic subjects and there were students enrolled heavily in vocational courses. Often, the two types were quite out of balance in a student's curriculum. Counsellors and vocational education teachers in the high schools I visited told me that it would be very difficult—indeed, virtually impossible—for students emphasizing vocational studies to shift into an academic concentration and graduate in the normal time. In effect, there is in most of the high schools in our sample an academic track and a vocational track.

The second provision for diversity is found within the academic offerings. Eight of the thirteen schools were tracked in the four subject fields usually required for college admission (mathematics, social studies, science, and English); the remaining five schools were tracked in three of these subjects. A major assumption underlying tracking has been the need to separate slower and faster students into different *levels* of the subject matter so that the bright students would not be slowed by the less able. (Although this assumption has been brought into question by research, it tends to persist.) But, in our sample of schools, this assumption has been expanded far beyond its traditional meaning. Commonly, we found students to be tracked not only into different levels of the same subjects but also into different subject matter. That is, those in the lowest tracks frequently were engaged in subject matter not previously encountered by students now in the upper tracks. Conversely, those in the upper tracks frequently were studying subject matter to which those in the lower tracks would not be exposed at some later time. Tracking, then, was not just in *level* but in *kind* of subject matter.

Ironically, in the name of individual variation, these schools may be giving up on individuals too soon, tracking them into self-fulfilling prophecies of low-paying jobs. Needless to say, many individuals so tracked will live lives that defy such prophecies, but they often will do so in spite of rather than because of their education in schools.

Most of us who pushed vigorously during the 60's and 70's for individualized learning had in mind the need to address the wide range of student attainment in any class of "graded" students—a range spanning about four grade levels at the fourth grade and increasing steadily with upward progression through the school. A major task for curriculum developers, we reasoned, was the identification of fundamental elements (concepts, principles, skills, values, and the like) to be learned by all students *commonly* but at different rates of speed. It would be necessary, we thought, to employ a variety of teaching techniques and, perhaps, even to differentiate for students of varying abilities the topics used for the ultimate mastery of these subject matter elements. But few of us had in mind accounting for human variability by separating students into differing streams of knowledge. This certainly is not what Bloom[4] envisions in his proposals for mastery learning.

What we hoped for—and what the Project on Instruction set out to stimulate—was to link the growing understanding of people and learning with subject matter in organizing curriculums and in teaching. This goal remains elusive; its implications should be at the top of our educational agenda.

Again, data from "A Study of Schooling" illuminate the problem. From questionnaires filled out by students and from extensive classroom observations, it becomes apparent that the range of pedagogical procedures employed, particularly in the academic subjects, is very narrow. As in most classrooms observed in our earlier report *Behind the Classroom Door,*[5] the teaching observed in our current study was characteristically telling or questioning students, reading textbooks, completing workbooks and worksheets, and giving quizzes. This pattern became increasingly dominant with the progression upward from primary to secondary classes. Sadly, there were few signs to suggest increased efforts to reach slow learners in the lower tracks through more creative, nurturing pedagogy. Indeed, such evidence as there was to suggest imaginative teaching turned up somewhat more frequently in upper or advanced subject matter tracks.

In general, there were differences in teaching between the academic subjects as a group and the arts, physical education, and vocational/career education. In the latter cluster of subjects, teachers were less likely to be sitting or standing at the front of the room; students were less likely to be reading textbooks or completing workbooks. Teachers tended to "tell" less and demonstrate or show more. They and their students tended more often to be doers together; students in these subjects participated more frequently in planning learning activities. The "flatness" characteristic of so many classrooms observed, particularly among those above the fourth grade, was noted less among classes in these subjects. When asked to rate the subject fields in terms of their interest, students consistently chose the arts (first at all levels), physical education, and vocational/career education ahead of the academic subjects. It would be a mistake to conclude that differences in teaching alone accounted for these ratings. Many other explanations come to mind. But it would be equally unwise to reject this explanation.

It would be a misinterpretation to assume from preceding paragraphs that the academic subjects should be taught in a fashion similar to the arts, vocational education, and physical education. The point to be made, rather, is that if students are to learn, they must become engaged with the subject matter, whether it is a mathematical problem, the characteristics of some other culture, the shaping of clay, or the structure of a poem. This engagement does not occur similarly for all kinds of learning; nor does it occur similarly for all individuals, whatever the subject matter. A concept needs to be read about, talked about, written about, perhaps danced or acted out, and eventually used in some meaningful context.

But the forms of enticing the necessary engagement appeared to be limited in the classrooms of our sample, to become established by the upper elementary years, and to become rigid with upward progression. Of course, there were exceptions. Some teachers deviated from the pattern. But even in the arts, a considerable portion of the teaching was characterized by the kinds of activities described earlier as dominating the academic subjects. And although the teachers in our sample subscribed overwhelmingly to the importance of praise and encouragement in the learning process, we found little of it in the classroom. Further, the incidence of such teacher support declined steadily from the primary grades upward.

By the time the students in our sample were a few years into the dozen years of elementary and secondary schooling, daily life in school appeared not to be providing many surprises. Nor did we hear as we walked down the corridors those "belly laughs" Ole Sand said should emanate regularly from classrooms. But this does not mean lack of engagement in and with the place of their schooling. School is where their friends are. In responding to the question "What is the one best thing about this school?" the most frequently chosen answers at both junior and senior high levels were "my friends" and "sports activities." The "classes I'm taking" and "teachers" were relatively infrequently chosen categories. When asked who were the most popular students, "athletes" and "good looking kids" accounted for 60 percent of the junior high choices and a whopping 78 percent of the senior high choices. "Smart students" accounted for about 14 percent of the choices at the junior high level and only 7 percent at the senior high level. Smart students apparently fare better in the peer group environment if they are also good looking athletes.

It would appear that our secondary schools are faced with a momentous challenge in seeking to engage the young in academic, intellectual pursuits. Large segments of our data suggest not only a declining engagement from primary to secondary grades but also a decline, or at least a levelling off, in pedagogical approaches designed to increase the appeal of academic learning. And another part of our data reveals a steady decline in students' academic self-concepts (e.g., feeling good about their schoolwork) with upward progression through school.

As a nation, we have been markedly successful in getting into schools a large percentage of school-age children and youth. But unless we are markedly more successful in involving young people in the learning activities that schools presumably should provide, we can expect this percentage to decline. The question arises as to whether we can make universal schooling work—especially if we believe that universal schooling means not only schools commonly attended but also things commonly learned.

TOWARD COMMON LEARNINGS, UNCOMMONLY TAUGHT

The National Committee for the Project on Instruction assumed a society that values both unity and diversity. The challenge it posed was the designing of instructional programs to develop the individual potentialities of all members of the school-age population within this framework of values. For me, one implication to be drawn from "A Study of Schooling" data is that the schools in our sample recognize diversity by providing a varied curricular menu but a relatively unvaried pedagogy. I would argue for the reverse: a relatively common curricular fare but maximally varied teaching methods.

Students from diverse backgrounds should be enrolled together in common learnings taught through ways deliberately designed to recognize and appeal to their individual learning styles and abilities. In addition, part of each student's program should be uncommon, designed to develop some unique talent or capability and to use all the educational resources of the community. The ratio of learnings engaged in commonly to those studied uncommonly might well be about nine to one in the primary years and decline steadily to about seven to three in the senior high school years.

Our concern for individuals as persons must push us away from giving up on their potential and depriving them of options by tracking them early into self-fulfilling prophecies involving limited expectations. Our concern for individuals as citizens and for a democratic society's need for educated citizens must push us away from segregated tracks for different "classes" of learners. The work of the common school—a school commonly attended, with things commonly studied but uncommonly taught—is not finished. Indeed, our schools have been through a bulge in the enrollment of diversity. The challenge now is to educate this varied student population commonly.

The challenge comes after what has been a depressing decade for educators and schools. The back-to-basics movement has spoken to diminished curricular expectations and the lowest common denominators in teaching, not to comprehensive educational programs for all and innovations in teaching.

As we move through the 80's, however, there are some encouraging signs. More and more thoughtful people are coming to realize that mechanistic, rote teaching encourages mechanistic learning and not problem-solving ability and other complex, cognitive processes. Data from "A Study of Schooling" show that the parents studied in the sample want a full range of intellectual, social, vocational, and personal educational goals for their children. This should not surprise us. One is forced to wonder why we did not assess parental wishes more carefully before embarking on a course of diminished expectations.

The tasks of curriculum conceptualization and development are awesome. What constitutes a K–12 program designed to develop, in balanced fashion, the intellectual, social, vocational, and personal abilities of all children and youth? What organizational arrangements are most likely to assure sequential progress through such a program? What help and support must teachers receive if they are to be highly successful in engaging diverse groups of students in common learnings? What are the prospects for mobilizing community resources to provide the instruction and the role models needed for the development of unique, individual talents? And how can federal and state agencies be truly helpful to local schools in assuring both equity regarding access to knowledge and high-quality delivery systems?

Most of these questions were posed by the National Committee for the Project on Instruction at the beginning of the 60's. They were neglected in the 70's. They now provide the curricular and instructional agenda for the 80's. Let us not allow lesser questions to push these aside.

REFERENCES

1. Sand, Ole, in the preface to: Fraser, Dorothy M. *Deciding What To Teach;* Goodlad, John I. *Planning and Organizing for Teaching;* and Miller, Richard I. *Education in a Changing Society.* Washington, D.C.: National Education Association, 1963. (All volumes in the series were produced by the Project on the Instructional Program of the Public Schools.)

2. For further information on the Study and the sample, see: Goodlad, John I.; Sirotnik, Kenneth S.; and Overman, Bette C. "An Overview of 'A Study of Schooling'." *Phi Delta Kappan* 61: 174–178; November 1979.

3. Conant, James B. *The American High School Today.* New York: McGraw-Hill, 1959.

4. Bloom, Benjamin S. *All Our Children Learning.* New York: McGraw-Hill Book Company, 1980.

5. Goodlad, John I.; Klein, M. Frances; and others. *Behind the Classroom Door.* Worthington, Ohio: Charles A. Jones, 1970.

CHAPTER 8

Instructional Imperatives for the 80's

Geneva Gay

Back to the basics . . . Minimum competency testing . . . Violence in the schools . . . Declining enrollments . . . Student apathy . . . Spiraling costs . . . Declining standardized test scores . . . Busing . . . Equity and equality in educational opportunities . . . Global citizenship . . . Lifelong learning . . . So goes the list of issues and concerns of prime importance to American educators during the decade of the 80's.

While the issues of concern to educators are numerous and varied, parents and the public seem particularly distressed about the levels of student competency in two areas considered essential: literacy and marketable job skills. The underlying assumption is that, upon completion of their formal schooling, individuals must be able to communicate and to compute at certain levels of proficiency, as well as to earn a living, if they are to compete in a world of advancing technology, inflationary economics, and high rates of unemployment.

Current school programs seem to be designed particularly to help students develop skills at the most basal level. This emphasis, undoubtedly prompted by prevailing societal conditions, translates into programs that stress fundamental literacy skills such as reading, writing, and arithmetic; saleable skills for the economic marketplace; and functional skills such as balancing a checkbook, filling out application forms, and practicing wise consumerism. Conditions of learning are also increasingly restricted to the bare basics. Innovative and experimental teaching techniques and learning environments are progressively minimized.

Ideologically, these shifting educational emphases and approaches give pre-eminence to *functionalism* and *vocationalism* in all school programs, regardless of the particular subject matter. That is, more often than not the merits of instructional content and activities are determined according to their *direct* potential for increasing the learners' chances of getting and/or maintaining a job. This functionalist, vocational focus, with its emphasis on skills training, permeates all levels of education from the primary grades through post-graduate studies. Students are socialized throughout their schooling experiences to conform to existing norms; to behave in certain ways; to adopt certain attitudes and behaviors; to study hard and be punctual, respectful, and dependable; and to value particular subjects or courses because "they are good preparation for when they enter the work world as full-time employees." School programs have become more committed to preparing students for restrictive, predetermined, and narrowly defined roles than to educating them for a wide range of options and alternatives in an ever-changing world. As a result, education today is "little more than training for the industrial army."[1]

While necessary, mastery of basic skills and vocational competency are *not* sufficient to adequately prepare today's youth for effective social–civic participation and for maximum personal fulfillment in the complex, technologically sophisticated world in which they must live. Unquestionably, the young need to acquire proficiency in basic literacy skills. But to limit educational programs to these is, at best, to equip students with only the barest minimum of capabilities. At worst, such emphases will sentence youth to guaranteed adolescence; they will make them into psychological and intellectual cripples who have not developed the kinds of skills, orientations, attitudes, and habits of mind necessary to continue to grow, to engage in self-renewal when necessary, and to keep pace with a world that is in a perpetual state of change.

NEEDED: EDUCATION FOR REVITALIZATION

The learning experiences and program priorities more likely to serve the needs of youth in the 80's are the ones less liable to receive great popularity in the current educational climate. These are the more experiential, affective-based, process-oriented programs that are more difficult to translate into immediate performance indicators, and, thus, the results are more difficult to measure. The effects of such educational experiences may not become apparent until long after students have left the classroom. Schools must, thus, reassess their missions, restructure their ways of operating, and recommit their programs to helping students develop attitudes and skills that transcend present realities. School programs must also be reordered to give greater attention to the "hows" and "whys" of issues, circumstances, and events, as opposed to the prevailing emphasis on the "whats" of life situations.

The greater challenges of the 80's will center on "people and process problems," as opposed to the concerns of the last few decades that focused primarily on production, technological developments, and the conquest of nature.

> The great question of these times is how to live in and with a technological society; what mind and what way of life can preserve man's humanity and his very existence against domination of the forces he has created.
>
> . . . .
>
> What we need is education that will enable us to make use of technology, control it and give it direction, cause it to serve values which we have chosen.[2]

Most assuredly, acquiring a narrow range of vocational skills and attitudes and mastering the most rudimentary literacy skills (through modes of instruction that place students in passive roles) are inadequate preparation for facing such a challenge. Instead, a more plausible approach might be to use experiential learning techniques, experimentation and confrontation ideologies, and process-oriented goals and objectives. The list of appropriate goals should include self-understanding, the capability to cope with change, critical thinking and decision-making abilities, interpersonal relations and communication skills, the capacity for self-education, and tolerance for ambiguity. Together these goals define the contours of *education for revitalization,* a fitting agenda for American schools in the 80's.

John Gardner's description of the "self-renewing individual" incorporates the major skills and attitudes one needs to possess to continue to grow personally and intellectually, to *revitalize* himself or herself, and to maintain individual and social vitality and versatility in a world of perpetual changes and challenges. The self-renewing person is one who possesses self-understanding; has the curiosity to try and the courage to fail; is willing to commit himself or herself to certain convictions; understands the interactive relationship between the development of self and society; is open-minded, versatile, and flexible; is a creative and critical thinker; and has a tolerance for uncertainty and ambiguity.[3]

Education for revitalization—the capacity to renew and update one's interests, potentialities, and skills as necessitated by changing circumstances and desires—is especially important for developing skills that will be functional beyond the immediate present for three crucial reasons.

First, in order to make any sense of all the diversified and often conflicting information and stimuli to which individuals are exposed, they must have greater understanding of their own strengths and weaknesses; their levels of tolerance–intolerance; their values, beliefs, roles, and functions; and the interrelationships between the self and its various environments. This self-understanding or self-realization is fundamental, given that:

> Human beings have always employed an enormous variety of clever devices for running away from themselves, and the modern world is particularly rich in such strategems. We can keep ourselves so busy, fill our lives with so many diversions, stuff our heads with so much knowledge, involve ourselves with so many people and cover so much ground that we never have time to probe the fearful and wonderful world within. More often than not we don't want to know ourselves, don't want to depend on ourselves, don't want to live with ourselves. By middle life most of us are accomplished fugitives from ourselves.[4]

For individuals living in a world in which human beings and human interactions are increasingly relegated to second place status behind machines and technology, the temptation to become even further alienated from self and from others will increase instead of decrease in the future. The tendencies already in motion that dehumanize, depersonalize, alienate, and isolate individuals in a crowded world are likely to become even more commonplace. If what psychology tells us about the effects of negative self-concepts and identity crises on the psychological well-being of individuals and on the way they live their lives is so, then educators must plan instructional experiences to counterbalance the negative effects of technology and industrialization on both society and the individual. One such emphasis should be education for the rediscovery of self and its liberation from the domination of technocracy.

A second reason for school programs to educate for revitalization in the 80's is, as Charles Reich would say, to avoid preparing youth for a living death.[5] That is, persons who acquire a fixed set of attitudes and skills that are resistant to frequent modification, who cannot deal with the complexities of life, and who cannot keep pace with the changes that occur will exist, but not live. Medically alive, they are psychologically traumatized and sociologically dysfunctional. Such individuals constitute a vast human wasteland. Consequently, both the general potential and the overall quality of every individual, as well as of society, are minimized.

We know that with the present rate of medical improvements, most children will live healthier and longer lives than their parents. Transportation and communication changes will make them world citizens. It will be as easy to travel from New York to Cairo as from Boston to Denver, and events occurring in Jerusalem will be as easily accessible as those happening in Chicago. Industrialization and automation will be such that individuals will change jobs four or five times during their lifetimes. The eight-hour workday and the forty-hour workweek may become obsolete. The average person can expect to live much longer; to interact with a much wider, more diversified range of peoples and experiences; to move about the country more easily, freely, and often; and to have a great deal of leisure time at his or her disposal. Change will be the most consuming characteristic of his or her life.

What is the school to do to help youth develop the skills and attitudes that will serve them well throughout their life histories of changes, contrasts, conflicts, and unanticipated directions? The answer is embedded in the notion of education for perpetual revitalization. That is, schools must create habits of mind and of being whereby one is always ready to confront change, to regroup, to rechannel and reorder priorities. Self-vitalizing individuals have the capacity to cope with unforeseen challenges, to tolerate internal conflict, and to suspend judgment while engaging in social experiences and interpersonal interactions. They are not traumatized by unanswered questions or unresolved differences. Nor do they find it hypocritical or unduly distressing to express opposite sides of their being (the conscious and the unconscious, the rational and the passionate, the structured and the spontaneous, the intuitive and the scientific) at the same time.[6]

The classroom should become a laboratory in living, a societal microcosm wherein the context, content, and techniques of teaching and learning more closely resemble the world at large. Students should experience various educational arrangements in the classroom. This can be facilitated if teachers exhibit greater flexibility and use more imagination in establishing grouping patterns that employ various interest, ability, age, grade, and task combinations. Cooperative student exchange programs within and between school districts are another possibility. These activities will provide students with opportunities to *experience* diversity in environments, values, and peoples; to make choices and decisions and then know the consequences of the actions taken; to confront change; and to develop meaningful relationships with others.

Far more learning situations should be created wherein students are simultaneously exposed to multiple, conflicting stimuli; wherein several, equally appropriate and attractive options are available; wherein problems without apparent solutions are presented; wherein value conflicts occur; and wherein no directions are provided except those that are offered by the students themselves. Teachers should deliberately cultivate classroom environments and relationships with students wherein *everything* that is said and done, both by students and by teachers, is subject to question, inquiry, and critical analysis. The idea of semester- or year-long schedules should cease to exist; rather, school and classroom schedules should be changed frequently, *and* without any particular form of regularity. Students must be challenged to confront themselves—their biases, values, beliefs, expectations—and others. They should study ethnically, culturally, and nationally diverse peoples, experiences, events, and heritages. There should be frequent opportunities for students to decide *what* they will study and *how* these studies will be conducted.

Much more attention must also be given to action-based learning, or learning by doing, within the context of cooperative group efforts. In other words, students must learn through experience that there is value in cooperating with diversified others to attain mutually beneficial goals, and that individual fulfillment and group achievement are frequently interactive. Timidity, fear of failure, or a demand for guaranteed success as a precondition for undertaking a learning challenge must be replaced with a healthy sense of curiosity and daring and a willingness to undertake a challenge for its own merits. Thus, school programs should strive to achieve what Charles Reich, in *The Greening of America,* calls "education for consciousness." Programs committed to education for consciousness encourage and socialize the student to always—

> . . . question what he is told and what he reads. . . . demand the basis upon which experts or authorities have reached a conclusion. . . . doubt his own teachers. . . . believe that his own subjective feelings are of value. . . . make connections and see relationships where the attempt has been made to keep them separate. . . . appreciate the diversity of things and ideas rather than be told that one particular way is the "right" way. . . . be exposed and re-exposed to as wide a variety of experiences and contrasts as possi-

ble. . . . learn to search for and develop his own potential, his own individuality, his own uniqueness.[7]

Diversification, exploration, experiencing, and experimentation in a context of flexibility and change should be the pivotal descriptors of school environments and programs implemented in the 80's. The advice of René Dubos on regaining the significance of humanity in a progressively technicized world is equally apropos as educators establish the instructional agenda for the 80's. He says,

> . . . we must shun uniformity of surroundings as much as absolute conformity in behavior and tastes. We must strive instead to create as many diversified environments as possible. Richness and diversity of physical and social environment constitute an essential criterion of functionalism whether in the planning of cities, the design of dwellings, or the management of individual life.[8]

In many ways technology has revolutionized communication and brought the world within arm's reach of most Americans. This same technology that makes a global culture feasible also tends to insulate people, isolating them from each other and prohibiting substantive interpersonal interaction and communication. When exposed to human values, behaviors, problems, and experiences they do not understand, too many Americans tend to retreat into the protective cocoons of their own cultural biases and ethnocentrism. Mass media confront the individual with a wide array of life options, information, choices, and consequences, all of which must be analyzed, screened, and assigned meaning as they relate to personal desires and aspirations. Without adequate communication skills, youth are liable to be overwhelmed by the bombardment of information and become easy prey for indiscriminate propagandizing. This, then, is a third reason for instructional programs to give priority to education for revitalization. If, indeed, the greatest challenges of the next few decades are going to be people- and process-oriented, then knowing how to communicate with and relate to others is fundamental to the nurturing of human potential as well as to the revitalizing of each individual.

While it is true that such geographically distant places as China, Saudi Arabia, and Australia are not beyond the reach of Americans, many youth still have strong ethnocentric attitudes about ethnically different peoples, both at home and abroad. Differences are very intimidating. Yet, population growth and technology are, in effect, making the world smaller each day, thereby forcing ethnically, racially, and culturally different peoples into closer proximity. The time is rapidly approaching when there will be no place to run to avoid people, values, and experiences that threaten us. Individuals will have to take a stance, to deal with these diversities, and to interact with many different kinds of peoples. The psychology of identity tells us that individuals' senses of self and personal worth are largely reflections of how they think others perceive them and of the quality of their interpersonal relationships. Impressive technological improvements in communication are not enough to adequately prepare youth to form fulfilling interpersonal relationships in the 80's. "The pursuit of significance is bound to fail unless man learns once more to speak to man."[9]

School programs must reconceptualize the teaching of reading and writing as the teaching of communication skills. Defining and teaching reading in the 80's in much the same ways as they were done in the 50's is ridiculous. Today's youth are children of technology. They do far more visual and audio reading than their parents ever imagined possible. Yet, too many school programs continue to give primary attention to "mental reading" (i.e., correctly recognizing words, and their meanings, on a printed page). Given people's growing dependence on audio and visual mass media for information, it is more practical for reading instruction to enlarge its emphasis to include development of selective listening and critical viewing skills. Far greater use should be made of video and audio tapes, photography and graphics, and disc recordings in reading instruction. And students should learn such skills as interpretation, word usage, and comprehension as much from looking at and listening to people's expressive behaviors in a variety of settings and situations as from reading printed materials.

Furthermore, it is not unthinkable that in the near future computers will become as commonplace as communication devices as radios, televisions, and telephones are today. Soon every home will be equipped with a computer. School programs should, therefore, include skill building in computer programming and in the use of the computer for information storage, retrieval, and exchange on their instructional agendas for the 80's.

Effective communication skills go far beyond mastery of reading and writing. In the best sense, they include engaging in active interchanges with others, knowing how to listen, recognizing common bonds between self and others, understanding and appreciating people and experiences for who and what they are, and recognizing that divergent attitudes and behaviors are the modes through which the richness of humanity is expressed. School programs designed to equip students with attitudes and skills that will facilitate meaningful relationships and effective communication should examine (1) the needs and means of acquiring abilities to differentiate communication styles according to the characteristics of participants and events; (2) the nuances of communication behaviors and how these are differentiated according to time, place, and people (gestures, voice tone, word choice, signs and symbols, protocols, etc., differ according to such contextual factors as culture, ethnic group, geographic locality, time era, social class, educational level, and purpose or function of the communication act); (3) different written and spoken forms of communication, as well as symbolic language and nonverbal factors; (4) various communication genres such as kinetics, dance, drama, song, poetry, oratory, advertising, art, and photography; (5) vocabulary and other communication behaviors that are alienating and facilitating in cross-cultural interactions; (6) the factors and circumstances that give rise to new words and cause others to become obsolete; and (7) the interactive relationships among communication abilities; personal fulfillment, achievement, and recognition; and the capacity for societal and individual revitalization. Students should be very much aware of the power of persuasion, the potential of subliminal suggestion techniques used by mass media to influence individuals, and the devastating effects that inappropriate communication behaviors can have on international, interpersonal, and cross-cultural relationships.

CONCLUSIONS

Educating youth for the 80's is an astronomical task. The challenge is to develop attitudes and to teach skills; to encourage habits of being and behaving that will serve the demands of the here and now, and yet transcend the boundaries of the present and remain useful in the uncertain future. This task is made even more difficult because many of the established precedents and priorities in educational practice are no longer functional or dependable guidelines for action. And the specific characteristics of the future are more unpredictable than ever before. Most assuredly, though, to limit school programs in the 80's to emphases on cognitive mastery of basic literacy skills and vocational skills would have tragic ramifications for the youth and for the nation's future. While necessary, these skills and conditions of learning are not sufficient to adequately prepare young people to be vital and versatile throughout their lives, which will be lived in a world of unprecedented and unpredictable change.

A more plausible approach to providing students with an education that has both functionality in the present and the inherent capacity for perpetual revitalization to meet future demands is to give priority to the processes of self-education. The self-educating, self-renewing, revitalizing learner develops habits and skills in thinking critically, choosing from among an abundance of options, coping with change, achieving self-understanding and self-reliance, tolerating ambiguity, establishing meaningful relationships with diversified others, working cooperatively for the attainment of group goals, and constantly regrouping and reallocating personal resources and expectancies to keep attuned with a changing world. Neither life's conditions nor students of the 80's will demand or settle for less from the instructional programs offered by our schools. The extent to which the potential of each individual is nurtured and repeatedly revitalized is the degree to which society, too, remains vital and creative. Conversely, to minimize individual fulfillment is to diminish societal viability.

REFERENCES

1. Reich, Charles A. *The Greening of America.* New York: Random House, 1970.

2. *Ibid.* pp. 17 and 358.

3. Gardner, John W. *Self-Renewal: The Individual and the Innovative Society.* New York: Harper and Row, 1964.

4. *Ibid.* p. 13.

5. Reich, Charles A. *op. cit.*

6. Gardner, John W. *op. cit.*

7. Reich, Charles A. *op. cit.* pp. 359–360.

8. Dubos, René. *So Human An Animal.* New York: Charles Scribner's Sons, 1968. p.175.

9. *Ibid.* p. 158.

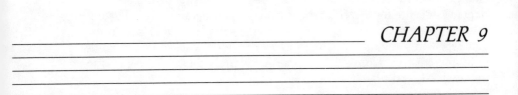

CHAPTER 9

Facing Up to Educational Equity

Lois A. Martin

Educational equity will be a primary national concern for at least the remainder of this century. Schools must strive to assure that all students have the opportunity to succeed in programs that challenge them and to participate fully in the life of the school. Fulfilling this goal is one of the greatest challenges schools have ever faced. We must eliminate not only sexism but also other types of educational inequity: racism, ageism, and the discriminatory treatment of students who have physical or mental handicaps or who have ethnic or religious backgrounds different from the school majority.

Public schools have not always had, or taken the responsibility, to ensure that girls and boys have life opportunities that are not circumscribed at birth. As educators become aware of sexism and find ways to overcome and prevent it, they become increasingly sensitive to other forms of bias and increasingly skilled in improving the human condition.

Each societal change brings changes in the schools; some are embraced, while others are resisted. Until recently, changes in the roles of women and men and, therefore, in the education of girls and boys have been neither resisted nor embraced. In fact, they have not been consciously noted. Yet, they are occurring. To remain unconscious of them is to resist them. Educators in the 80's must increase their awareness of societal changes and of the possible range of school responses to them.

Educational equity for girls and boys requires attention to four things: (1) equal access to school activities and instructional programs; (2) opportunities for full participation in those courses, activities, and groups to which one has been admitted; (3) opportunities for maximum achievement, according to one's potential; and (4) the expectation that school achievements will be valuable, thus motivating both girls and boys to set short- and long-range goals and ensuring that these goals are worthwhile.

We live in a society with stereotyped sex roles. The first question we ask upon the birth of a child is "Is it a boy or a girl?" The answer affects everything from what gifts the child is likely to receive to what expectations the parents have for the child's future. Nursery rhymes teach children that little boys are made of "rags and tags and old paper bags." While that's not very complimentary to boys, such ingredients at least convey the impression of practicality. The "sugar and spice and everything nice" that little girls are made of implies something less— or more—than necessary.

School programs reflect society's understanding of the present and its vision of the future. Students who enter kindergarten in the 80's will live their adult lives in the twenty-first century. While the students in our schools in the 80's need to become strong, moral, resilient, intelligent, diligent, knowledgeable, competent, and caring adults—time-honored traits—they will carry out their roles as workers, parents, and community members in ways different from those portrayed for adults in most of today's curriculum.

In each decade, developments in science and technology have changed the nature of work both in the marketplace and in the home. Most jobs no longer require sheer muscular strength, and labor-saving devices and products have eliminated the need for full-time attention to household operations.

"The old order changeth Yielding place to new," wrote Alfred Lord Tennyson in 1842, at the beginning of the scientific and technological revolution. "And God fulfills Himself in many ways, Lest one good custom should corrupt the world." How can "one good custom . . . corrupt the world"? What once-accepted practices have vanished for the public good? Slavery, indentured servitude, and primogeniture have disappeared, but they once seemed right to most people. The traditional differentiation of sex roles with their concomitant stereotyping of females and males enabled an agricultural economy to flourish and lay foundations for the modern world. In the 80's to promote or even unwittingly to accept without examination the sex role differentiation of the past as part of the educational program is to teach students about a present that does not exist and to prepare them for a future that will never come.

Profound changes in the workplace and in the family have taken place in the last quarter century and are expected to continue. These changes—more two-parent families with both parents as wage earners and more single-parent families—are occurring most rapidly among the young, the poor, and the urban populations. However, the trend applies to all social, economic, and age groups in the country. In fact, the greatest change in the past decade in participation in the labor force is for women (with husbands and children) in middle- and high-income brackets. In the 70's they became wage earners at a faster rate than did low-income women in the 60's.

Traditional roles for women and men have always been exaggerated. In the past, women were field hands—in fact, field slaves—and worked in factories and mines. Women ran shops and operated farms without the assistance of husbands. Men on the frontier in early America knitted on long winter days and nurtured plants and animals. They raised families alone as widowers or deserted spouses.

Yet, girls and boys are barraged with messages that set stereotyped expectations for their behavior. Recently, I saw an ad in a magazine that offered posters titled "Why God Made Little Boys" and "Why God Made Little Girls." The illustrations and the text on the posters show that boys climb mountains, sail the seas, explore unknown lands, and climb trees. Girls, on the other hand, dance and sing, gather flowers, and commune with nature. Boys obviously rise to the challenges of the world while girls are onlookers.

Both girls and boys need to be courageous, energetic, brave, curious, strong, sensitive, and joyous. Both need to conquer new worlds and appreciate the virtues of the ones they are in. Schools need to help them do that.

Yet, sex-role stereotyping in the instructional program gives girls and boys unfair and inaccurate ideas about themselves. It deprives them of the freedom to find their own places in society according to their capabilities by casting them into an apparently inflexible world. It limits their chances of becoming the women and men they are capable of becoming because it engenders feminine and masculine patterns of behavior that do not reflect reality.

Schools, and society, are filled with sexism. Children label some of their male classmates "sissies" and some of the females "tomboys." Parents are told in conferences, and sent messages on report cards, that

90

their daughters are "charming" and their sons "will be boys." Girls are "quiet" but boys with the same behavior "don't relate to their peer group." Conversations in faculty lounges and counselors' suites reinforce conclusions about children and their families based on sex-role stereotypes. Billy, for example, is hard to handle because he lives with his mother and "everyone knows" a woman can't discipline an adolescent boy. The child who receives such commendations or admonitions soon learns to conform to what is expected because of her or his sex. And both sexes are ascribed socially acceptable and unacceptable roles.

Sex-role stereotyping begins with inaccurate information and false assumptions about the differences between females and males. Such stereotyping leads both girls and boys to reach conclusions about themselves that are not true and that are unfair to them because they reduce their confidence in themselves and limit their life choices.

As an example of how this works, let's look at how real physical differences between "average" women and "average" men often lead to assumptions about all females and all males that are not true and that do injustice to both.

The average adult male is taller and heavier than the average adult female. That appears to be genetically determined. Accepting that as a fact does not mean that it is correct to assume that all normal males are, in fact, taller than all normal females. Statistics describe groups, not individuals. It is tyranny for students to believe that the midpoint in a frequency distribution is normal and that everything else is not. It is rank discrimination to class all members of a group with some imaginary average measure for that group. Adolescence would be less traumatic for most girls and boys if our educational program dealt realistically with the wide range of characteristics that are normal for females and males.

Another form of stereotyping is the generalization from one characteristic to another. Because the average adult male is taller than the average adult female, it is not correct to assume that males are more intelligent, physically healthier, or more stable emotionally. Neither is it fair to assume the opposite because twice as many men as women commit suicide, twice as many men as women have ulcers, and men have shorter life expectancies and more heart attacks than women. Instead of proving male deficiencies, these facts appear to be evidence that society places stress unequally on the sexes.

One of the most thorough studies of sex differences, *The Psychology of Sex Differences* by Eleanor Maccoby and Carol Jacklin, reports very few biologically based differences between females and males but many culturally ascribed ones.[1] Even scientific data collection may be influenced by sexism, according to reports of recent research conducted at the National Zoo. Women scientists observing and analyzing data on animal behavior have produced evidence that challenges theories about the physiological makeup and social roles of females and males in given animal species. Men observing animals failed to identify the characteristics of females of a species that were noted by the women scientists. Female and male scientists appear to watch animal behavior from different perspectives. "If you write something from a female bias, it really sticks out," a female scientist told a reporter from *The Washington Post,* "but if someone writes from a male bias, it's hard to pick it out unless you are sensitized to it."[2]

We need instructional programs that deal objectively with the differences between females and males and with the reasons for those differences, some of which are genetic but more of which appear to be culturally determined. We need an instructional program that points out not only the range of differences within female and male groups but also the many similarities among human beings, regardless of sex. Students need accurate information and explanations about human characteristics and behavior, not stereotypes.

Instructional materials often treat sex differences in a didactic, romanticized, and out-of-date way. Since most American women are wage earners at some time during their lives, textbooks are hardly realistic when they show mothers at home all day and fathers as the sole wage earners.

Not only does the content of instructional programs and materials present inaccurate or misleading information about females and males and the roles of women and men, but also our language and our idioms further reinforce stereotypes. The English language, like many others, is sexist. "Man" can mean an individual male or all of humanity. "He" can mean an individual male, anyone in a group, or someone of unknown sex. Since most people interpret most words literally and not generically, the world seems overwhelmingly male.

What sex comes to mind with each of these terms: countryman, craftsman, draftsman, flagman, forefather, freeman, journeyman, marksman, middleman, salesman, showman, statesman, upperclassman, shipping boy, yes-man? Pretty clearly male, aren't they?

Terms for males are usually more complimentary than those for females. Consider "brave" and "squaw," "wizard" and "witch," or "bachelor" and "old maid." Our language implies not only that males predominate numerically but also that they are more valued than females.

Illustrations in books and other visual aids reinforce the sex-role stereotypes our language conveys. In career education materials, relevant occupational attributes such as clothes and functions are invariably attached to irrelevant ones such as sex, age, and race. Hard hats and the operation of heavy equipment are attached to young males. Aprons and pie baking are attached to elderly females. Problem solvers in mathematics and science are male; assistants are female. However, some improvements are being made.

Federal legislation is forcing change in many areas to bring about greater equality of opportunity for Americans, regardless of race, national origin, religion, age, sex, or handicapping condition. Title IX of the Education Amendments of 1972 is the major legal constraint on sexism in the schools. In 1976 the Education Amendments to the Vocational Education Act established specific sex equity requirements for vocational programs.

However, custom continues even after laws change requirements. As educators we must examine our knowledge base and our educational programs and practices to make necessary improvements. We must ensure that students are given the opportunity to prepare for the variety of roles women and men share. Most adults are householders, wage earners, spouses, and parents. Both women and men are consumers and citizens, and have intellectual, emotional, and physical dimensions. Yet, ideas regarding sex differentiation in these roles continue to be communicated to children. Boys are guided toward occupational planning so that they can become wage earners, and girls are taught in home economics how to be consumers.

Sexism is unfair to both girls and boys, now as well as in future roles. Much has been written about books that invariably show girls or women in passive roles and boys or men in active roles; that show girls as onlookers and boys as doers; that show girls as cautious and boys as willing to take risks. Generally these analyses are presented to show that such books are detrimental to girls. But they are also detrimental to boys. They don't show boys curled up in chairs, basking in the pleasure of reading. They don't show men working at typewriters, or with books, paper, and pencils. They communicate to boys that they must be aggressive and physically active. No wonder so many more boys than girls have reading problems and difficulty in concentrating on schoolwork— apparently a feminine rather than a masculine endeavor.

Sexism has many ill effects. It hampers or prevents schools from fulfilling their mission to prepare all students to participate successfully in society and to guide our nation toward greater democracy and strength. Sexism prevents students from taking full advantage of the curriculum. It discourages free selection of those courses that prepare students for a wide range of vocational and avocational activities by guiding them into those expected to interest girls or boys. When all students do study the same subjects, sexism leads to differences in motivation and achievement. Finally, expectations set by sex-role stereotyping in society and reinforced by the school lead to discipline problems and a whole range of academically nonfunctional behaviors.

What can the schools do to help girls and boys develop their own capabilities now and plan realistically for their futures? First, we must reach a consensus about the importance of eliminating sex-role stereotyping. Second, educators must recognize not only the many forms that sex-role stereotyping takes in our schools but also its consequences. Third, we must remove, prevent, or offset such stereotyping.

A nonsexist school is one dedicated to the goal of educational equity for female and male students. Such equity requires equal access to instructional programs and school activities, equal resources for programs and activities in which girls and boys cannot participate together, and equal opportunities for achievement. *Equal access* requires that students receive objective information about themselves, that the curriculum be responsive to societal and personal needs of students, and that the students be motivated through guidance and the climate in the school to take full advantage of the curriculum. *Equal resources* means that courses or activities that may, for one reason or another, continue to be single-sex or predominantly female or male must receive equally competent instruction, appropriate materials and equipment, and equal expectations and commendations for achievement. But most important is assurance of *equal opportunity for success.* If both girls and boys are to achieve to their fullest potential, courses and activities must present content that is neither "feminine" nor "masculine" in its appeal. Instruction must be provided to compensate for out-of-school learning that makes girls and boys better able to take advantage of some school activities, such as crafts for girls and sports for boys. Instructional materials and classroom practices must be examined to ensure that they do not reflect intimidating sex-role stereotyping—e.g., that girls who excel in auto mechanics are not fully feminine or that boys who are dancers are not fully masculine. Adequate role models—in life, print, and visual materials—must be provided to motivate both girls and boys.

Here are steps that schools for the 80's should take to ensure sex equity:

1. Analyze—and, if necessary, revise—the curriculum to stress the rights and responsibilities of individuals as family members, community members, producers of goods and services, consumers, citizens, spouses, parents, friends and—simply—

human beings. Emphasize the present as well as future roles of children and youth. Make sure that the school itself is a setting in which the student learns and can exercise her or his rights and responsibilities as a community member, producer, and consumer—and not merely as a female or male.

2. Identify and emphasize the competencies necessary for students to function effectively in a variety of present and future roles. These competencies include the acquisition of knowledge that enables human beings to deal with ideas. Teach students how to maintain or increase competencies, how to acquire additional competencies, and how to continue acquiring throughout life those new competencies needed or desired. Stress that *functional* is not minimal, but rather it describes a level of achievement appropriate for a purpose. For many purposes, society demands very high levels of competence. Full use of human faculties and full development of girls' and boys' potentials require a commitment to excellence in education. School is not a spectator sport; neither is it a menu from which students pick minimum daily requirements. Meaningful educational equity for girls and boys in this complex society requires that schools make a greater commitment to intellectual, physical, and emotional development.

3. Improve access to activities and courses. First, analyze the participation of females and males in courses and activities. Then remedy any imbalances. Publicize the fact that courses and activities are open to all students. Recruit students to participate in those activities that are imbalanced. Change course titles and content to make them equally appealing to both sexes. Remove course titles such as "Bachelor Living," which implies that an unmarried male is helpless and that the course is for boys only.

Communicate information about job opportunities or personal uses of a subject or activity. Provide information to overcome low achievement expectations for one sex (such as in mathematics or interscholastic athletics in the case of girls) or low interest expectations for one sex (such as in home economics or office occupations in the case of boys).

At all school levels, work with parents to help them understand the opportunities available to their children. Make parents aware of sex-role stereotyping and what they can do to help overcome it. In the middle or junior high school years, involve parents in planning for their children's high school programs. By the end of the eighth grade, see that each student has an educational plan for grades 9 through 12 and beyond that has been worked out by the student, counselor, and parents. Open high school classes to parents of students in the lower grades so that they can see how a daughter might fare in an electronics program or a son in cosmetology. Have secondary students who are enrolled in classes or involved in activities not traditional for their sex talk to their peers at class registration time or to students at lower grade levels about their experiences and plans.

4. Organize, formally or informally, a research and information service on sexism for the school staff. Let the staff know about current periodicals with articles that may be of interest to them regarding educational equity for girls and boys. Circulate new pamphlets and reports as they are received. Increase awareness of ways to promote educational equity for girls and boys in the development and administration of policies, in classroom instruction, in the awarding of honors, in the assignment of tasks, and in the coverage of student accomplishments.

5. See that all staff members know about Title IX of the Education Amendments of 1972 and about the guidelines for its implementation, including institutional self-evaluation. See that it is implemented in spirit as well as in the letter of the law. Have an affirmative action plan for the instructional program as well as for improving balance in staffing, and get regular progress reports.

6. Develop a plan of action to remedy sex inequities in carrying out school routines, disciplinary actions, and other activities. List all of the aspects of school life that should be examined; then collect and analyze data, set goals, and note progress. Do girls collect papers in classrooms and accompany hurt children to the health room? Do boys operate audiovisual equipment and move book collections? Are boys suspended from school and girls merely told not to behave that way again?

7. To ensure full and equally worthwhile participation of both girls and boys in instructional programs, establish guidelines for nonsexist instruction and use them to plan course content. The guidelines should include the following points: (a) females and males should be represented in approximately equal pro-

portions; (b) both females and males should be treated as competent and successful workers who make significant contributions in and out of the home; (c) both females and males should be treated as possessing the full range of physical and behavioral characteristics that they, in fact, have.

8. Set guidelines for nonsexist instructional and counseling materials, and use them for selecting new materials and culling existing collections. Consider the illustrations as well as the story or factual content. Are females and males accurately represented? Is coverage balanced? Are sex roles incidental or central? Check the guidelines of publishers, school systems, and state departments of education, and those published in professional journals to make sure that yours are comprehensive and workable.

9. If the only materials available are sexist, learn how to recognize the slant and remedy the bias. Note the omission of females and males and any distorted information about either sex. Note the tendency to generalize from one particular difference between a female and a male to all females and males. Discuss with students the possible reasons for distortions and omissions and the ways in which they could be remedied. Examine with students any inferences that may be made when materials include terms that have both specific and generic meanings.

10. Make a checklist and survey materials collections and displays in media centers, guidance offices, and classrooms. Remedy deficiencies. Are there areas marked "for girls" or "for boys"? Are both men and women treated adequately in social science, science, and history collections or displays? Is there an adequate number of biographies of women and reference materials that can be used to supplement those textbooks in mathematics, history, and other subjects in which almost all people mentioned are male? Do displays, posters, and prints show women and men favorably in roles other than traditional female and male ones? Do career education materials suggest a wide choice of vocations for students rather than listing options separately for girls and for boys? Do media displays and activities sponsored by the guidance department increase student awareness of sexism and sex-role stereotyping in school and society?

11. Give special attention to career education. Invite community members who are not in sex-role stereotyped occupations or

activities or who have occupations that have been stereotyped for the other sex to meet with students. Provide students with up-to-date information about job prospects. Remember the original meaning of *career:* the course of one's life. That includes not only wage earning but also responsible participation in the family and the community. A proper balance in those roles is becoming available to both women and men, and should be planned for in the educational program.

Revise the curriculum to include public policies and legislation that affect the lives of women and men, both as wage earners and as family members. See that both teachers and students use current information as well as forecasts about the economy, scientific and technological advances, work opportunities, family life, and community activities.

Include in the media center and guidance offices self-administered and -scored interest inventories and other skills-assessment materials. Arrange field trips and community-based career education programs, such as student-volunteer internships in workplaces or contacts with adults who will work as mentors to assist students in independent study or career planning.

12. Provide role models within the school to help both girls and boys set nonsexist expectations for themselves. Does your school have male secretaries, parent volunteers, classroom aides, cafeteria workers, and kindergarten teachers? Does it have female bus drivers, coaches, custodians, science teachers, and administrators?

13. Plan for regular in-service training of staff to increase awareness of sexism and skill in overcoming it. Work in grade-level or departmental groups, or as whole school staffs, to learn how to recognize sex-role stereotyping and how to eliminate it in ways that have positive effects on students and staff.

14. Depending upon the school level, set up staff–student–parent discussion groups. See that the school community keeps informed about how society is changing, what is causing change to occur, and how change affects the lives and choices of students. Establish parent education and outreach programs to help parents set nonsexist expectations for their daughters and sons.

15. Act to reduce the sexism communicated by the English language. Get the National Council of Teachers of English

"Guidelines To Encourage Non-Sexist Use of Language" or similar materials available from publishers and professional associations, and put them into practice. Use neuter terms such as "people" instead of generic, but also masculine, ones such as "all men." Avoid patronizing terms for females ("the fair sex" instead of "women") and sex-stereotyped nouns and adjectives ("co-ed" instead of "student"). Treat men and women with the same linguistic respect.

REFERENCES

1. Maccoby, Eleanor, and Jacklin, Carol. *The Psychology of Sex Differences.* Stanford, Calif.: Stanford University Press, 1974. 2 vols.

2. Crosby, Thomas. "Women Researchers Find It's an Animal 'Queendom.' " *The Washington Post,* February 27, 1978. pp. A1 and D12.

CHAPTER 10

The Impact of Technology on Curriculum
W.C. Meierhenry

Technology is believed to be the driving force behind social change. In the last 30 years, there have emerged a number of superindustrial societies, including the United States which is in an era characterized by large-scale modern enterprises and their impact on the external social and physical environment. The next 100 years may well be a time of transition into the postindustrial society stage, which refers to a very affluent economy that meets its industrial and material needs with a small percentage of its workforce and economic effort.

Most economists and futurists believe that the 1980's will be the watershed period between the last several decades, in which vast quantities of cheap energy fueled an average annual growth rate of about 5 percent in industrialized nations, and the next couple of decades, which will probably see annual growth rates of 2 to 3 percent. Since a great deal of the past growth in government budgets, including funds for schools, was made possible through the annual growth of productivity, it is evident that a 2- to 3-percent growth rate will have a significant impact on social institutions, including schools.

In spite of a possible decrease in growth of the economy for the decades ahead, such futurists as Kahn and Phelps at the Hudson Institute believe that the next 10 to 20 years will be a period of continuing explosive progress in the informational technologies and that computers will be a major factor in changing from a service-oriented society to one in which much more activity will be accomplished by machine.[1] Thus, even though there probably will be a slowdown in most dimensions of the economy in the next few years, it is predicted that technology will continue to grow.

Another way of viewing the short-term future is offered by Wedemeyer and others who believe that the world is entering an *information* or *communication age:*

> The world is entering an era that will most probably be referred to as the "information" or "communication age." The world economic order has apparently been shifting (since about 1970) from an industrial base to an information base. One of the primary driving forces of this new order is the rapid convergence of telecommunication systems and the computer.
>
> This shift has been described by many including Fritz Machlup (1962) in his analysis of the knowledge sector of the U.S. economy, Daniel Bell (1976) and Peter Drucker (1969) in their early work on the "post-industrial" or "knowledge-based" society, and, most recently, Marc Porat (1977) in his work on the emerging information economy. Each of these authors has pointed out that we are leaving an order characterized by industrial production, which was energy- and materials-intensive, and entering a new world order based upon the creation, storage, manipulation and dissemination of information, which is communication-intensive.
>
> Work now underway at Harvard's Information Resources Program is based upon the notion that information is one of three "basic" resources—along with materials and energy. Just as materials and energy are potential resources, that are of no practical use in the "pure" state, information has no value without being "put to work." Information is made operational through communication: communication, then, can be referred to as a "kinetic resource"—information at work.[2]

What does all of this have to do with education? Several things—for example, education and instruction have a close relationship with communication. In fact, Edgar Dale once said that good communication is good teaching.[3] While learning requires more than good communication, effective communication is a necessary base for learning. Also, schools need to alert students to the future they will likely inherit, which will be technologically based. Finally, educators must utilize the power and variety of these newer instructional technologies.

What reason is there to believe that schools will make greater use of instructional technology than they have in the past? One major factor referred to earlier will be the continuing short-fall in terms of financial resources to support schools because of lower productivity. Coupled with this factor are the following: the labor-intensive nature of the present school system and the impact that inflation will have on its cost of operation. For example, if double-digit inflation of around 14 percent continues, school budgets will need to be doubled in the next five years in order to provide the same services as they do now. With all the other demands on the tax dollar at all levels of government, it is not likely that there will be a doubling of current school budgets in the next five years. It is clear, therefore, that both the size and the nature of public education will have to change.

At the same time that costs are escalating for human services, the cost of technology is decreasing. One of the reasons for such dramatic decreases is that those technologies that use circuitry profited from the invention of the chip (which can be mass produced for a few cents and which can provide for integrated circuits consisting of hundreds of thousands of components). The first microprocessor chip introduced in 1972 contained about 5,000 components, while a chip produced in 1978 contained about 18,000 components on an area one-half centimetre square (0.2 square inch). What has happened as a result of this one invention has been a 10,000-fold increase in performance for the same cost. This means that in 1978 a few hundred dollars bought the equivalent computing power that required several million dollars in the mid-1950's. At this rate long before the decade is over it will be possible to purchase for less than $200 a pocket-size computer that is faster and has more memory than the most powerful computer in the world in 1979.

Similar progress is being made in such telecommunications services as telephone, radio, and television. Telecommunications, which is the substituting of electrons for paper, began in the 1850's with the telegraph. By 1870, the telegraph had captured 10 percent of all communication revenues in the United States; by 1900 telephone and telegraph accounted for 30 percent, and sometime in the late 1950's, telecommunication captured more than 50 percent of communication revenues. The estimate is that by the year 2000, 75 percent of communication revenues will be captured by telecommunications. In addition, other examples could be cited as evidence of how the various technologies will impact on society generally as well as on education specifically.

In addition to the cost advantage discussed above, several factors suggest a penetration of technology into the schools of the future that is faster than in the past. First, many of the technologies used in schools are not under government regulation. Baer has pointed out that had the calculator industry been regulated by a government agency, we might still be waiting for the delivery of complex computers rather than buying $9.95 electronic calculators at the supermarket.[4] Although certain dimensions of telecommunications, such as telephone and television, have been under government regulation in the past, there is increasing evidence that there will be less control in the future. Another factor is that technology moves and is accepted most rapidly where it is an add-on feature to current technologies rather than a completely new invention. Instructional technologies of the 80's are likely to be supplemental to current devices rather than replacements.

THE IMPACT ON CURRICULUM

It is evident that the various technologies used singularly or in combination will have strong impact on the school curriculum of the future. Some predictions have been made by Dede as to the possible impact of technology on education:

Given that we are intelligent enough to use instructional technology wisely, what will be its long-term net effects? One eventual outcome may be that training ("limited range of right answer" learning) will be almost completely done by machine, while educating ("multiple right answer" learning) will be facilitated by people. This implies that subjects such as reading and basic math may be machine taught, while areas such as creative writing will continue to be conveyed by human instructions.

A second long-term effect may be that new definitions of intelligence will emerge. Historically, our definition of intelligence has changed based on our technological capabilities. For example, fifty years ago, having a near photographic memory was an important part of being intelligent because the kind of rapid data retrieval that we have now was not available; today, memory is less important to intelligence. Similarly, as machines are developed with instructional skills, different human capabilities will be seen as indicating intelligence.

To work with others using machines as intermediates, new types of communication skills will be necessary; we may see innovative communications styles that will allow us to be person-oriented and affective even when sending messages via the computer or television. After all, this is what a good media personality is able to accomplish; we may study Johnny Carson to learn the way he communicates sociability, social presence, and affect over the air waves, how he compensates for the loss of direct contact that takes place when machines mediate communication.

A third outcome may be that everyone in society will have a

better understanding of the strengths and weaknesses of technology because all of us will be interacting with technology day-to-day, learning from and programming machines. We may become more intelligent and sophisticated in using technology when we continuously see what it is and is not capable of accomplishing.[5]

Using the computer as one example of technology, Roland suggests its application in addressing the fundamentals:

> For those concerned about "getting back to basics" in education, a strong microcomputer-based program is likely to be the answer. Computers force people to do things right. They impose a very valuable discipline on the way people perform. They are impartial, instructive, and demanding. Students cannot get by without paying attention. The student interacts with the instructional computer in an active way that sustains interest and improves the rate and quality of learning. The program can adapt itself from second to second to the particular needs of each student and can identify problems that may require the intervention of a human teacher, social worker, or medical worker.[6]

In addition to the general curricular implications of technology, there are implications particular to all subject matter areas.

Mathematics

With the development of the microcomputer, mathematics became a field that has many immediate applications. Although calculators and microcomputers will be used for many of the basic mathematical calculations, mathematicians feel that there will always be a need for students to perform the four fundamental operations accurately. The calculator and microcomputer will make possible, however, the development of problem-solving skills because they allow a shift of emphasis from computational activities to the intricacies of problem solving.

Modern mathematics anticipated some of the new technological developments and helped students to understand and apply the binary unit (number base of 2). But with the demise of the new mathematics, the curriculum moved away from such concepts as the use of different number bases. These concepts need to be reintroduced. Attention also needs to be given to matrices since such understandings are needed to utilize the computer. The mathematics classroom of the future surely will include a laboratory with calculators and microcomputers available.

Social Science

Because of the implications of energy shortages, inflation, and population increases, social science teachers will need to understand and utilize calculators and microcomputers to aid in various future projections. Social science teachers cannot leave to mathematics teachers the interpretation of these statistical trends, and will, perhaps, have to master the skills for computing various statistics. Television reception directly by satellites from anywhere in the world will enhance the teaching of the social studies at the macro level. The use of the television "porta pak" by individual students or classes will permit the capturing of scenes from the local community for classroom analysis, discussion, and possibly action at a micro level.

Science

Because science, especially physics and chemistry, involves mathematics, it is clear that the calculator and microcomputer will play large roles in this subject in the future. Advancements in photography, such as the new spectrometer at the University of Chicago, make possible the study of the movements of the various elements of the atom. Science students in the future will be able to see and observe such things as organs of the human body and the far reaches of the universe because of new generations of motion picture and television cameras and transmission systems. Thus, new technologies will open up new worlds for science students.

English and Communication

Even the English program will feel the effects of technology, according to Jennings:

> The illogical spelling and grammar rules of standard human speech and writing have proven to be the major stumbling blocks in attempts to produce accurate machine translations from one human language to another or to phrase precise instructions for a computer in "natural" English. Increasing dependence upon computers is likely to produce modifications in human languages that will make them less inconsistent in spelling, grammar, and meaning so that the same written text or spoken phrase will be equally comprehensive to man and machine.[7]

The above examples are only suggestive of the changes that will occur in the future curriculum of the schools. As various technologies are further developed and utilized by creative teachers, even more extensive changes will occur in the content that is taught, and also these changes will produce the need for much more interdisciplinary work.

POTENTIAL TECHNOLOGIES FOR EDUCATIONAL USE

Considerable reference has been made already to various communication technologies. Emphasis in the future will be on using various technologies in tandem and in combinations. At this point, technologies will be discussed individually, even though they will be utilized most often in combinations in the future.

Television

Television will not be thought of as a single-channel medium in the future. Cable television (CATV) with its multiple channels suggests the variety of programs and approaches that individual learners and teachers need and that can be delivered to them.

With the advent of direct broadcast from satellite to television receiver, the potential range of programs is increasing enormously. A recent advertisement in a Lincoln (Nebraska) newspaper quoted a price of $9,650 for a complete earth terminal for FM and TV. The advertisement indicated that the FCC had recently dropped any and all requirements for such television-viewing stations to be licensed, and that if one was a professional maintaining a license as a nurse, doctor, dentist, or realtor, the terminal could be a tax write-off for educational purposes. A conference held in Oklahoma City in the summer of 1979 was designed to assist individuals to build their own terminals for as little as $200.

Currently, there are about 20 commercial communications satellites in space, and there is a limit to the number of satellites that can be "parked" in orbit. It is possible, however, that technology may overcome these limits, and, if so, by the year 2000 there could be the equivalent of 22,000 TV satellite channels. There are hundreds of satellite terminals in use in the United States today (many by cable television systems), and, in the future, many school districts certainly will install their own terminals.

There are a number of developments under way to make the individual television screen much more information-rich in terms of technology. One of these developments is *teletext*, which is a device attached to the television set to store information transmitted between picture transmissions. Teletext enables the viewer to switch away from a television program and receive such information as news reports, the latest football scores, weather reports, current stock market reports, or recipes of the day. Special information for a particular audience can be sent by teletext—for example, in Kentucky a "green thumb box" (a small, 12-key computer terminal) is providing farmers with market prices, crop reports, weather forecasts, and other information upon a spin of a telephone dial and the touch of one of the green thumb buttons. Thus, the television screen becomes a potential source for massive amounts of information. In some instances, as in the example cited above, a telephone line can be used to gain access to a computer, with the information being displayed on the television screen.

Another way in which the television set can be made more responsive to user needs is through the use of videotape recorders. Many schools have found that if they record programs on videotape, they can then play back the programs to meet the needs of students and teachers at the most appropriate time; open circuit television is used only as a delivery system.

One of the technologies just coming on the scene, which also uses the television set, is the video disc. There are several types of video disc machines under development, but one on the market has 54,000 single images on a disc the size of an ordinary stereo record. Each of the 54,000 frames is numbered, and some models enable one to retrieve a specific frame with a minimum search time. It is also possible to regulate both forward and reverse speeds when displaying individual pictures. If the video disc is connected to a microcomputer, the search capabilities are enhanced, and it is possible to program individualized instruction.

Telephone

The telephone has many capabilities not utilized fully by education. Although telelecture and blackboard-by-wire installations have been available for some time, additional uses exist for the telephone. A 12-key pushbutton telephone can serve as a low-cost intelligent terminal if there is added to it a microprocessor and associated memory, a slot for a magnetic card or some other simple data-entry device, and a liquid crystal readout. The telephone could access not only voice libraries of recorded information for instructional purposes but also data bases.

Another change will be the transmission of data in digital form (binary units as used by computers) rather than analog (voice transmission). The telephone system will be used extensively for the automatic (as opposed to the manual or verbal) transfer of data. It will make possible the direct connection of the telephone with computer terminals and facsimile transmission machines instead of requiring conversion devices as is now the case.

Although optical fibers are not likely to replace copper wires for cross-country telephone lines, the technology is being used in Atlanta, Chicago, and New York. An optical fiber consists of a core of transparent glass coated with a more reflective glass. A beam of light entering the fiber will travel along it with very little loss of intensity. Because the principal raw material for making optical fibers is ordinary sand, they will be far less costly to manufacture than are today's copper cables. The most important feature of the optical fibers, however, is their enormous carrying capacity since a single fiber one-fifth the thickness of a human hair can do the work of 10,000 ordinary telephone wires or can serve as a television station transmitting 8,000 different channels at the same time. Optical fibers will make possible the transmission of many more messages at much lower costs.

Instructional Calculator

Another instructional technology already used considerably in education involves the portable computer/calculator/microprocessor necessary to accomplish semisophisticated computer-assisted instruction. According to Dede, the instructional modes that can be programmed on inexpensive but powerful calculators include the *tutorial approach* (the computer presents simple material, asks questions to determine proper assimilation, and corrects misunderstandings), the *inquiry approach* (the student asks for a specific fact, and the computer responds with appropriate data), the *dialogue approach* (the student asks a general question, and the computer responds with a complex answer), and the *explanation/interpretation approach* (the computer presents complex learning material and responds to general questions).[8]

Long before the end of the 80's, a *dator* (a word used by Swedes for both computers and terminals) is likely to be a pocket-sized, hand-held device which will unfold to reveal an alphanumeric keyboard, flat color screen, speaker, microphone, video camera, and receptacles for plugging in small mass modules. Some dators may be small enough to be worn like wrist watches.

CONCLUSION

Education is in the unique situation: technology needs to be used by educators in planning and designing instruction; and learners need to be able to use the technology employed in connection with their own learning, and to master the same or similar technologies for present and future uses. There are various predictions about the impact of technology on our society and its educational institutions. Wedemeyer suggests the impact of technology on communications as a factor:

> New communication services are emerging out of the convergence of computers and telecommunication networks that provide the technological infrastructure for the new world communication order. Already in more developed countries there has been a shift from an industry-based economy to an information-based economy.
>
> The expansive and instantaneous nature of these new networks will create new communication careers and change the nature of society. . . . Those who have access to or control of these network services will have the power to change the nature and function of offices, postal services, banks and a host of other social/cultural institutions.[9]

Choosing one technology—the computer—Roland indicates something of the changes for the workforce and some of the principal obstacles to widespread use of the microcomputer by everyone including teachers:

> Contemporary society is facing the greatest occupational upheaval in history, and we need to plan for it. Many people will emerge from this upheaval permanently unemployable, and society must find ways of distributing the produce of the economy on some basis other than productivity, or else let a substantial part of the population starve. At the same time, there will be a critical shortage of advanced skills, most of them associated with microprocessors and their applications. There will be a need for the entire population to be computer-literate and unless such literacy is imparted from early childhood, a substantial part of the population may find that they lack the basic skills to get along in their daily lives.[10]

And finally Dede indicates an initiative that all of us should assume:

> . . . anticipatory social inventions to regulate the use of instructional technologies; to reduce the negative effects that they may produce, and increase the receptivity of teachers and administrators to machines as a means of reducing costs. To accomplish this, we need to reconceptualize the training that we give teachers and administrators, to develop alliances with media associations and computer associations, and to explore creative ways to raise capital so that we can invest in these technologies without being saddled with too heavy a debt.

Taken as a group, these three immediate agendas illustrate an approach pioneered by British economist E. F. Schumacher known as "appropriate technology." Schumacher's strategies for managing technology are designed to minimize the negative side effects so often associated with increasing reliance on machines. Education's chances of a bright future are much higher if we anticipate the challenges these new technologies may pose than if we wait and find ourselves in a reactive, crisis-oriented posture.

We are facing a period in education similar to the introduction of the printing press 500 years ago. Before that time, those people who could read (a small percentage of the population) used a few hand-copied manuscripts as their source of information; for the rest of the populace, recitors and actors conveyed ideas orally. In converting to the printing press, people faced problems similar to those discussed here: a loss of human factor, new skills required and valued abilities suddenly made obsolete, career shifts, massive needs for capital investment, etc. But, although decades passed before books were used to their full educative potential, the shift to the printed word for information dissemination ultimately did result in progress, increased learning, and exciting new frontiers for education.

Recent technological advances pose a similar opportunity for us. The traditional teacher is in a position analogous to that of clerks after the end of World War II, when the computer was developed. Suddenly, many fewer clerks were needed—but new, more interesting jobs were available for skilled personnel. We can be similar to monks copying manuscripts by hand while the printing press makes us obsolete, or we can be in the forefront by simultaneously developing instructional technology and retaining traditional educational approaches where appropriate.[11]

Education in the 80's stands at a crossroad. There is no turning back, and the most feasible and rational choice to make in order to serve the needs of learners and to maintain some semblance of the present school system is to utilize instructional technology as an integral part of all levels of education in the future.

REFERENCES

1. Kahn, Herman, and Phelps, John B. "The Economic Present and Future." *The Futurist,* June 1979. pp. 202–222.

2. Wedemeyer, Dan J. "New Communications Services for the Future." *World Future Society Bulletin,* January–February 1980. pp. 1, 6. Reprinted with permission of the World Future Society. See also:
Bell, Daniel. *The Coming of the Industrial Society.* New York: Basic Books, 1976.

Drucker, Peter. *The Age of Discontinuity*. New York: Harper and Row, 1969.

Machlup, Fritz. *The Production and Distribution of Information in the United States*. Princeton, N.J.: Princeton University, 1962.

Porat, Marc U. *The Information Economy*. Special Publication 77-12. Washington, D. C.: U.S. Department of Commerce, Office of Telecommunications, 1977.

3. Dale, Edgar. *Audiovisual Methods in Teaching*. Revised edition. New York: The Dryden Press, 1951. p. 9.

4. Baer, Walter S. *Telecommunication Technology in the 1980's*. Santa Monica, Calif.: The Rand Paper Series (P-6275), 1978. pp. 3, 54.

5. Dede, Christopher J. "Educational Technology: The Next Ten Years." *World Future Society Bulletin*, November–December 1979. p. 6. Reprinted with permission of the World Future Society.

6. Roland, Jon. "The Microelectronic Revolution." *The Futurist*, April 1979. p. 89.

7. Jennings, Lane. "The Human Side of Tomorrow's Communication." *The Futurist*, April 1979. p. 108.

8. Dede, Christopher J. *op. cit.* pp. 3–4.

9. Wedemeyer, Dan J. *op. cit.* p. 6.

10. Roland, Jon. *op. cit.* p. 90.

11. Dede, Christopher J. *op. cit.* p. 7.

CHAPTER 11

Multiethnic Education and School Reform
James A. Banks

THE NEED FOR CONCEPT CLARIFICATION

A wide variety of concepts and terms in the educational literature relates to race, ethnicity, culture, and education. Among those currently in vogue are *multicultural education, multiethnic education, ethnic studies, cultural pluralism, bilingual–bicultural education,* and *crosscultural education.* There is much conceptual confusion in multicultural education, as in any emerging field. Concepts such as multicultural education, multiethnic education, and cultural pluralism are often used interchangeably or to convey highly similar meanings.

The wide variety of concepts in multicultural education reflects, in part, the conflicting policy recommendations being made by educators and social scientists who have different ideological commitments and, in part, the lack of consensus in the field about the goals that multicultural education should be designed to attain. A few educators and social scientists are strong cultural pluralists. They conceptualize the United States as a nation with tight ethnic boundaries, with each ethnic group championing its own political and economic interests and showing little concern for other ethnic groups or the nation state.[1] Other educators and social scientists are strong assimilationists who see ethnicity and

112

ethnic group characteristics as dysfunctional within a modernized democratic society such as the United States. They believe ethnicity is fleeting and temporary, and they endorse Robert E. Park's notion of ethnic group life in a modernized society. Park predicted that race relations would proceed through four inevitable stages: *contact, conflict, accommodation,* and *assimilation.* [2]

Another group of educational theorists endorses a multiethnic ideology.[3] They think that the strong pluralists and the staunch assimilationists conceptualize the nature of ethnicity in the United States inaccurately. The multiethnic theorists believe that ethnic youths are socialized to function both within their ethnic subsocieties and within the mainstream American society. Finally, the multiethnic theorists feel that the school should help individuals develop the knowledge, skills, and attitudes needed to function within their own ethnic group and within the universalistic American society, as well as within and across other ethnic subsocieties. I have called these skills, abilities, and attitudes *crosscultural competency.* [4]

In this essay, I will clarify the meanings of *multicultural education, multiethnic education,* and *ethnic studies,* and I will discuss the nature and characteristics of a multiethnic educational environment. I will conclude by suggesting ways in which you can, first, examine your school to determine the extent to which it is multiethnic and, second, plan strategies to make it more consistent with the ethnic and racial realities in American society.

Culture is the root of *multicultural.* Thus, a definition of culture will help us to clarify the meaning of *multicultural education.* Culture consists of the behavior patterns, symbols, institutions, values, languages, and other human-made components of a society. It is the unique achievement of a human group that distinguishes it from other groups within society. Since culture is a very broad and generic concept, we can define multicultural education as an educational reform movement designed to bring about equal opportunity for the wide range of cultural groups within a society. Because of past and present social, economic, and political conditions, many cultural groups in the United States are denied equal opportunities within the schools and in the larger society. Such groups include women, regional groups such as Appalachian whites, and groups that are heavily concentrated within the lower-class stratum of society.

An ethnic group has a shared history, common values, a sense of group identity, and other characteristics that differ from those of other groups within a society. *Multiethnic education* is a process designed to bring about changes in the total educational environment so that students from diverse racial and ethnic groups will experience educational equality. Multiethnic educational reform requires making changes in all aspects of the educational environment.

Ethnic studies is the scientific and humanistic study of the histories, cultures, and experiences of ethnic groups within a society. While ethnic studies is an integral part of both multicultural and multiethnic education, it is a more limited concept than either. Modernized ethnic studies programs are conceptual and interdisciplinary, and are designed to help students master higher-level concepts, generalizations, and theories. Such programs also help students to develop social action and social participation skills.[5] Table 1 summarizes the relationships among multicultural education, multiethnic education, and ethnic studies.

Since multiethnic education is a concept with wide boundaries, we must examine the total educational environment to determine whether a school is multiethnic. When I refer to a multiethnic school, I do not necessarily mean a school that has a multiethnic student or teacher population. Rather, I am referring to a school that has norms and values that respect and support the ethnic and racial diversity within American society. Many schools with ethnically and racially diverse populations are Anglo-centric in their norms, cultures, curriculums, and expectations. On the other hand, a few schools in predominantly all-white suburban communities reflect cultural diversity in their norms, curriculums, expectations, and policies.

It is important to emphasize that multiethnic education is a comprehensive concept that implies reform of the total educational environment. Many educators assume that multiethnic education involves only a superficial integration of the curriculum. Thus, they feel that multiethnic education has been implemented when they have added a few ethnic minority heroes to the Anglo-American heroes that are already studied. Such educators have misconceptions about both multiethnic education and modernized ethnic studies programs, which are conceptual and interdisciplinary and do not focus on isolated factual information about ethnic heroes.

MULTIETHNIC EDUCATION: A PROCESS

We must examine the total environment of a school to determine whether it is multiethnic and to what extent. Multiethnic education is an ideal-type conceptualization. It is an ongoing process that is never fully attained. Consequently, a school is never totally multiethnic, but rather it has achieved a degree or level of multiethnicity. It must con-

TABLE 1

PROGRAMS AND PRACTICES RELATED TO PLURALISM IN AMERICAN EDUCATION[6]

Program and Practice	Focus	Objectives	Strategies
Multicultural Education	Cultural groups which experience prejudice and discrimination in the United States	To help reduce discrimination against stigmatized cultural groups and to provide them equal educational opportunities To present all students with cultural alternatives	Creating an institutional atmosphere which has positive institutional norms toward victimized cultural groups in the United States
Multiethnic Education	Ethnic groups within the United States	To help reduce discrimination against victimized ethnic groups and to provide all students equal educational opportunities To help reduce ethnic isolation and encapsulation	Modifying the total educational environment to make it more reflective of the ethnic diversity within American society
Ethnic Studies	Ethnic groups within the United States	To help students develop valid concepts, generalizations, and theories about ethnic groups in the United States, to clarify their attitudes toward them, and to learn how to take action to eliminate racial and ethnic problems within American society To help students develop ethnic literacy	Modifying course objectives, teaching strategies, materials, and evaluation strategies so that they include content and information about ethnic groups in the United States

tinue to work to become more multiethnic in its values, pupil–pupil interactions, and student–teacher relationships.

To assess the level of multiethnicity of a school, we must examine many variables, including these: the motivational systems of students and those used by teachers; the attitudes, perceptions, beliefs, and behaviors of the school staff; the languages and dialects sanctioned by the school and those spoken by the students; the formalized curriculum and the course of study; the assessment and testing procedures used by the school; the school policies and politics; the school culture and the hidden curriculum; the counseling program; the instructional materials used; and the community participation in the school. Because of the limited scope of this essay, I will examine only several of these variables.

The Learning Styles, Motivational Systems, and Cultures of Ethnic Minority Students

A number of researchers have documented the mismatch of the primarily Anglo-centric learning environment of the school and the linguistic and cultural characteristics of ethnic minority students. The educational environments of most schools are more consistent with the learning patterns and styles of Anglo-American students than with those of ethnic minority students such as Afro-Americans, American Indians, and Puerto Ricans.

Some research suggests that the patterns of mental abilities differ among various ethnic groups. Stodolsky and Lesser studied four mental abilities (verbal ability, reasoning, number facility, and space conceptualization) among first-grade children of four American ethnic groups (Chinese, Jewish, Black, and Puerto Rican).[7] They conclude:

> . . . the most striking results of this study concern the effects of ethnicity upon the *patterns* among the mental abilities. . . . Ethnicity does affect the pattern of mental abilities *and, once the pattern specific to the ethnic group emerges, social-class variations within the ethnic group do not alter this basic organization.* [8]

Research also suggests that ethnic minority and Anglo-American students often differ in their cognitive styles and that most teachers have cognitive styles that match those of Anglo-American students. Ramírez and Castañeda have found that Mexican-American youths tend to be more field-sensitive than field-independent in their cognitive styles,[9] while Anglo-American students tend to be more field-independent. Field-sensitive and field-independent students differ in a number of behaviors and characteristics. Field-sensitive students tend

116

to like to work with others to achieve a common goal and are more sensitive to the feelings and opinions of others than are field-independent students. Field-independent students prefer to work independently and to compete and gain individual recognition. Students who are field-independent are more often preferred by teachers and tend to get higher grades.

Ethnic minority youths also differ from mainstream youths in their motivational systems and styles. Ethnic minorities such as Blacks and Chicanos tend to be more externally than internally controlled; Anglo youths tend to be more internally than externally controlled.[10] Students who are externally controlled believe that they can do very little to determine their success or failure because it is primarily determined by others. Internally controlled students believe that they can shape their own destiny. Most of the techniques used by teachers to motivate students are more effective with internal controlled students than with external controlled students. Thus, these techniques often fail to motivate ethnic minority students.

Often the tasks that teachers assign to ethnic minority students are nonmotivating to these students because they are inconsistent with the students' cultural norms, behaviors, and expectations. Teachers are frequently unaware of the cultural differences that their students bring to the classroom. Gay and Abrahams, as well as other writers, have described the cultural differences that minority youths bring to the classroom:

> Differences from Anglo-American middle-class culture run the gamut from different patterns of interaction, movement, socializing and growing up, to a distinct and highly flexible family and household system, religious perspective and practice, and so on.[11]

Problems often result when the teacher either fails to recognize the cultural differences of her or his ethnic students or interprets them inaccurately.

To work more effectively with multiethnic student populations, teachers need to participate in well-conceptualized staff development programs that will help them to acquire accurate knowledge about the cultural characteristics, learning styles, and motivational systems of ethnic youths and to master the skills needed to work more successfully with these youths. Techniques such as those developed by Longstreet might work successfully in training programs. To help her teacher education students become more sensitive to ethnic differences and use these differences constructively in the classroom, Longstreet taught them to carefully observe the ethnic behaviors of their students and to systematically record and interpret them: to develop what she calls an *ethnic profile* of each such student in their classroom.[12] The observation instrument that she gave her students consists of the following categories: nonverbal communication; orientation modes; verbal communication; social value patterns; and intellectual modes. We must be careful when training teachers to use this kind of observation instrument so that they will avoid overgeneralizing and creating new stereotypes of ethnic youths.

Teacher Attitudes, Expectations, and Behavior

A number of researchers have investigated teachers' attitudes toward and perceptions of ethnic and racial groups, and the effects that their attitudes have on students' self-concepts, attitudes, perceptions, and behavior. This research suggests that many teachers have prejudicial attitudes toward and perceptions of racial and lower socioeconomic groups, and that these prejudicial attitudes influence not only their verbal and nonverbal interactions with students but also student behavior and attitudes.

Rist investigated the grouping practices and interaction patterns within an all-black class during its kindergarten, first-, and second-grade years. The kindergarten teacher "placed the children in reading groups which reflected the social class composition of the class. . . . These groups persisted throughout the first several years of elementary school."[13] Rist concluded that a caste system existed within the classroom which reinforced and perpetuated the class system of the larger society. The teachers in the Rist study had apparently internalized dominant societal attitudes toward lower socioeconomic individuals and reinforced them in the classroom.

A monograph in the Mexican American Education study series indicates that teacher interactions with Mexican American and Anglo students exemplify an Anglo bias.[14] The categories in which this bias was statistically significant were (1) praising or encouraging, (2) accepting or using student ideas, (3) questioning, (4) positive teacher response, (5) all noncriticizing teacher talk, and (6) all student speaking. The monograph also indicates that Mexican-American students speak significantly less in class than do Anglo students.

Gay found that both black and white teachers interact differently with black and white students in desegregated social studies classrooms.[15] Teachers were more positive, encouraging, and reinforcing toward white students. White students also received more opportunities to participate in substantive academic interactions with teachers. Verbal interactions with black pupils were primarily nonacademic, procedural, critical, and nonencouraging. In an important study, Parsons found that a school he examined within a Mexican-American community reinforced the dominant societal attitudes and perceptions of Mexican Americans, and perpetuated the social-class stratifications that existed among Anglos and Mexican Americans.[16] Parsons concluded that the teachers were the primary socialization agents in the school that reinforced and perpetuated social-class and ethnic stratification.

The studies reviewed above indicate that many teachers have internalized the dominant societal attitudes and values toward minority and lower socioeconomic groups, and that they often reinforce these attitudes and values in the classroom. Regardless of their racial or ethnic group membership, teachers tend to internalize and perpetuate dominant societal values and attitudes toward racial and social-class groups. This research suggests that teachers must acquire more democratic attitudes and values before schools can practice social-class and cultural democracy. It suggests that staff development is needed to help teachers acquire the knowledge, skills, and attitudes needed to become effective multiethnic educators.

Multiethnic Testing

To make the school a truly multiethnic institution, major changes must be made in the ways in which educators test and ascertain student abilities. Most of the intelligence tests administered in the public schools are based upon an "Anglo-conformity, monocultural model."[17] Many students who are socialized within other ethnic cultures find the tests and other aspects of the school setting alien and intimidating. Consequently, they perform poorly on such tests and are placed in low academic tracks, special education classes, and low reading groups. Research indicates that teachers who teach in these kinds of situations tend to have low expectations for their students and often fail to create learning environments that will enable the students to master the skills and abilities needed to function successfully in society.[18]

Standardized intelligence testing, in the final analysis, serves to legitimize the status quo and to keep powerless the ethnic groups at the lower rungs of the social ladder. The results of such tests are used to justify the noneducation of minority youths and to relieve those who are responsible for their learning from accountability. We need to devise novel approaches to assess the abilities of minority youths and tests that will reflect the cultures in which they are socialized. However, it will do little good for us to create novel assessment procedures that reflect their cultures unless, at the same time, we implement curricular and teaching practices that are also multiethnic and multiracial. Students who score well on an ethnically oriented intelligence test are not likely to achieve well within an alien school that has a curriculum unrelated to their feelings, perceptions, and cultural experiences. Mercer has identified some changes that multicultural testing necessitates:

> A multicultural perspective would recognize the integrity and value of different cultural traditions. It would not assume that the Anglo-American culture is necessarily superior to other traditions, or that Anglo-conformity is imperative for social cohesion. It would accept the fact that there are multiple cultural mainstreams in modern America and that individual citizens have the right to participate in as many of these mainstreams as they wish. Differences in life styles, language, and values would be treated with respect, and persons from minority cultures would not be regarded as culturally disadvantaged, culturally deprived, or empty vessels.[19]

ASSESSING YOUR TOTAL SCHOOL ENVIRONMENT

In this essay, I have emphasized the need to examine the total school environment in order to (1) determine the extent to which it is multiethnic, and (2) plan and implement strategies to make your school more reflective of the ethnic and cultural diversity in American society. I have discussed only several of the school variables that must be examined when planning and implementing multiethnic educational reform —i.e., the learning styles of ethnic students, their motivational systems and culture, teacher attitudes and expectations, and multiethnic testing. Other important variables, such as language diversity, curriculum reform, and multiethnic teaching strategies,[20] were not discussed. However, I present criteria questions in Table 2 that can help you examine your total school environment to determine the extent to which it is multiethnic, and to plan and implement strategies to make it more multiethnic.

We can best view multiethnic education as a process, as well as a reform movement, that will help all students to experience equity and to develop the attitudes, skills, and abilities they need to function within and across different cultures—not only within this nation but also within our global society.[21]

TABLE 2
A Multiethnic Evaluation Checklist

Criteria Questions	Rating		
	Strongly ⟵————⟶		Hardly at All
1. Does school policy reflect the ethnic diversity in American society?			
2. Is the total school culture (including the hidden curriculum) multiethnic and multiracial?			
3. Do the learning styles favored by the school reflect the learning styles of the students?			
4. Does the school reflect and sanction the range of languages and dialects spoken by the students and within the larger society?			
5. Does the school involve parents from diverse ethnic groups in school activities, programs, and planning?			
6. Does the counseling program of the school reflect the ethnic diversity in American society?			
7. Are the testing procedures used by the school multiethnic and ethnically fair?			
8. Are instructional materials examined for ethnic and racial bias?			
9. Are the formalized curriculum and course of study multiethnic and multiracial? Do they help students to view events, situations, and concepts from diverse ethnic perspectives and points of view?			
10. Do the teaching styles and motivational systems in the school reflect the ethnic diversity of the student body?			
11. Are the attitudes, perceptions, beliefs, and behavior of the total school staff ethnically and racially sensitive?			

Criteria Questions	Rating		
	Strongly ←————————→		Hardly at All
12. Does the school have systematic, comprehensive, mandatory, and continuing multiethnic staff development programs?			
13. Is the school staff (administrative, instructional, counseling, and supportive) multiethnic and multiracial?			
14. Is the total atmosphere of the school positively responsive to racial, ethnic, and language differences?			
15. Do school assemblies and holidays reflect the ethnic and racial diversity in American society?			
16. Does the school lunch program prepare meals that reflect the range of ethnic foods eaten in the United States?			
17. Do the bulletin boards, physical education program, music, and other displays and activities in the school reflect ethnic and racial pluralism?			

REFERENCES

1. I discuss these various ideologies in considerable detail in: Banks, James A. "Pluralism, Ideology, and Curriculum Reform." *The Social Studies* 67: 99–106; May–June 1976.

Banks, James A. *Multiethnic Education: Theory and Practice.* Boston: Allyn and Bacon, 1981.

2. Coser, Lewis A. "Robert Ezra Park 1864–1944." *Masters of Sociological Thought.* Second edition. New York: Harcourt, 1977. pp. 357–384.

3. My own policy and curricular recommendations reflect the multiethnic ideology. See: Banks, James A. *Teaching Strategies for Ethnic Studies.* Second edition. Boston: Allyn and Bacon, 1979.

Banks, James A. *Multiethnic Education: Theory and Practice. op. cit.*

4. Banks, James A. "Shaping the Future of Multicultural Education." *Journal of Negro Education* 48: 237–252; Summer 1979.

5. See: Banks, James A. *Teaching Strategies for Ethnic Studies. op. cit.*

6. Banks, James A. "The Implications of Multicultural Education for Teacher Education." *Pluralism and the American Teacher.* (Edited by Frank H. Klassen and Donna M. Gollnick.) Washington, D.C.: American Association of Colleges for Teacher Education, 1977. p. 6.

7. Stodolsky, Susan S., and Lesser, Gerald. "Learning Patterns in the Disadvantaged." *Challenging the Myths: The Schools, The Blacks, and the Poor.* Harvard Educational Review Reprint Series, No. 5. Cambridge, Mass.: Harvard Educational Review, 1975. pp. 22–69.

8. *Ibid.* p. 43.

9. Ramírez, Manuel, III, and Castañeda, Alfredo. *Cultural Democracy, Bicognitive Development, and Education.* New York: Academic Press, 1974.

10. Vasquez, James A. "Bilingual Education's Needed Third Dimension." *Educational Leadership* 37: 166–168; (November 1979).

Vasquez, James A. "Motivation and Chicano Students." *Bilingual Education Paper Series.* Los Angeles: National Dissemination and Assessment Center, California State University, 1979.

11. Gay, Geneva, and Abrahams, Roger D. "Black Culture in the Classroom." *Language and Cultural Diversity in American Education.* (Edited by Roger D. Abrahams and Rudolph C. Troike.) Englewood Cliffs, N.J.: Prentice-Hall, 1972. pp. 67–84.

12. Longstreet, Wilma S. *Aspects of Ethnicity: Understanding Differences in Pluralistic Classrooms.* New York: Teachers College Press, 1978.

13. Rist, Ray C. "Student Social Class and Teacher Expectations: The Self-Fulfilling Prophecy in Ghetto Education." *Harvard Educational Review* 40: 411–451; August 1970.

14. United States Commission on Civil Rights. *Teachers and Students: Differences in Teacher Interaction with Mexican American and Anglo Students.* Washington, D.C.: U.S. Government Printing Office, 1973.

15. Gay, Geneva. "Differential Dyadic Interactions of Black and White Teachers with Black and White Pupils in Recently Desegregated Social Studies Classrooms: A Function of Teacher and Pupil Ethnicity." Washington, D.C.: National Institute of Education, 1974. pp. vii–x.

16. Parsons, Theodore W., Jr. *Ethnic Cleavage in a California School.* Doctor's Thesis. Stanford, Calif.: Stanford University, August 1965.

17. Mercer, Jane R. "Latent Functions of Intelligence Testing in Public Schools." *The Testing of Black Students.* (Edited by Lamar P. Miller.) Englewood Cliffs, N.J.: Prentice-Hall, 1974. p. 91.

18. Rosenthal, Robert, and Jacobson, Lenore F. *Pygmalion in the Classroom: Self-Fulfilling Prophecies and Teacher Expectations.* New York: Holt, 1968.

19. Mercer, Jane R. *op. cit.* p. 91.

20. For examples of multiethnic teaching strategies see: Banks, James A. *Teaching Strategies for Ethnic Studies. op. cit.*

21. This essay is based on material in the author's forthcoming book *Multiethnic Education: Theory and Practice.* Boston: Allyn and Bacon, 1981.

Pedagogically Sound Assessment
(Evaluation) Procedures

Bernard McKenna

PROLOGUE

The positions presented in this essay are based on the premise that all students, unless they are born with severe disorders of the central nervous system, are capable of learning, of accomplishing some things at a high level of proficiency, and of becoming involved in constructive, contributing, fulfilling enterprises. They are also based on the belief that the school needs to turn its attention to identifying interests, motivations, and commitments that can be developed in such ways that every student will eventually be evaluated as _successful._ Finally, they are based on the belief that these things can be accomplished if teachers and other professionals are afforded _few enough_ students and _time enough_ to identify and promote individual learning needs, interests, and motivations.

Those people, whether in or out of the teaching profession, who view these postulates as idealistic, as impractical, or as "pie in the sky" would do well to remember the words of William Carlyle: "Every noble work is at first impossible."

Certainly, such lofty ideals need to be considered in the light of the conditions in the society that might either promote or retard their soon being achieved. And since the conditions essential for achieving these ideals—*few enough* and *time enough*—are dependent on the availability of resources, the present adequacy and the future potential of resources need to be taken into account. That these ideals will be difficult to achieve should not deter those with deep beliefs and strong commitments from pursuing them.

THE SCHOOL CLIMATE

For the propositions set forth in this essay, school *climate* includes all those community, school system, building, and classroom characteristics, conditions, program content, and instructional processes that might be expected to mediate the accomplishment of agreed on goals and objectives for student learning, however the goals and objectives are articulated and however student learning is defined.[1]

In this sense, *climate* is a more generic term for what has been labelled in other places and by other observers as *conditions, inputs, resources, programs, processes,* and *strategies.* It is conceived as broad enough to include all these things that are believed to mediate, either intentionally or unintentionally, favorably or unfavorably, the accomplishment of goals and objectives. For example, *program* is often used as a way of defining those things that are believed to enhance processes and, consequently, to contribute to achieving goals and objectives: structural and administrative arrangements and activities, instructional strategies, and material resources. On the other hand, climate in this broad sense has to do with everything from community characteristics (deterring or enhancing), to the adequacy (or inadequacy) of financial provisions, to the sufficiency and appropriateness of a variety of print and nonprint materials for teaching beginning reading, to the processes by which reading is taught.

Types of Climate Evaluation

Although he seems to lean more toward the label *program,* House[2] has provided a useful delineation of types of climate evaluation. They are cited here as a basis for recommending what climate evaluation for the 80's should aspire to and be expected to achieve. Calling to attention the categories of models identified by House is useful for this purpose because the models display a continuum of points of view, articulating clearly differing philosophies as to the ends and means of evaluation. The categories of models identified by House are systems analysis, behavioral objectives, decision making, goal free, art criticism, accreditation, adversary, and transaction.

There are a number of possibilities for categorizing the models philosophically, operationally, and in terms of outcomes. They might be classified from quantitative to qualitative (as from systems analysis to art criticism). Or they might be categorized, as House does, from *objective* to *subjective* or even from *internal* to *external,* or they might be classified as *process* oriented as compared to *product* oriented.

This essay will not attempt to assess the characteristics and arguments put forth for the various models. House has accomplished this well. Rather, some principles will be set forth which, if adhered to, might result in climate evaluation's best serving its important purpose in the 80's. In doing so, the author's judgment is revealed on which model gives greatest promise for reflecting the principles identified.

The Main Purpose of Climate Evaluation

Several important purposes have been put forth in the literature for climate evaluation. Some of these are explicit in the titles given to the models cited above—for example, *decision making* and *accreditation.*

The main purpose of climate evaluation, as seen by this writer, is to determine which climate characteristics contribute most to improving learning opportunities and accomplishments for the students (who are, after all, the *raison d'être* for the entire education enterprise).

Once this determination is made, efforts should be continuously put forth to maintain and improve those characteristics.

Additional important purposes of climate evaluation include the following: (1) to reassure the public that the "education machine" is functioning effectively, efficiently, and economically; (2) to assist in decision making, in determining which climate factors must be maintained and improved and which must be replaced; (3) to establish policy on resource allocation; and (4) to advise professionals on correction of the process.

There are other purposes. But the central purpose, in the judgment of this writer, is the one on which is imprinted *student opportunities and accomplishments.*

Principles of Climate Evaluation

Whatever its purposes, the following principles need to be applied to climate evaluation for the 80's:

1. All stakeholders need to be involved in determining the purposes of particular evaluations and in agreeing to them.

2. All purposes that particular climate evaluations intend to serve need to be identified, clarified, and explicitly stated.

3. As criteria for evaluating climate, "opportunities" in the form of wholesome, healthful, democratic, and fulfilling processes should be as important as the student learning outcomes they are expected to foster.

4. School climate evaluation should take into account that different climates are appropriate for differing instructional purposes and expected outcomes.

5. School climate evaluation should take place primarily in naturalistic settings.

6. The study of school climate should move toward an ecological model along the lines articulated by Dawson, Tikunoff, and Ward[3]—that is, in evaluating climate the classroom should be looked on as a total ecological unit. Once it becomes possible to analyze and assess all the interactions among students, teachers, and the total environment of the teaching–learning setting, it will be time to include for consideration other building-unit systems and communitywide factors affecting teaching and learning.

7. Evaluations of school climate should adhere to *Standards for Evaluations of Educational Programs, Projects, and Materials.* These carefully worked-out standards for planning, conducting, and reporting evaluations were developed by a committee representing 12 national educational organizations. While the *Standards* are the first of their kind and will require continuous improvement and updating, they are now ready for use and promise to serve well the evaluation community in conducting future school climate evaluations.

8. Formative evaluations (evaluations conducted at intervals during the process in order to correct it) should so characterize and permeate all climate evaluations that once a program or project is concluded or at a stage for summative evaluation, a separate summation will be less needed because there will have been accumulated a continuum of data and judgments that displays the success of the program all along the way in accomplishing its intended final goals.

9. While emphasizing a multiplicity and a variety of criteria, evaluations should increasingly move toward those criteria in

House's list represented by *art criticism* and *accreditation*. The systems analysis model hasn't worked well for the private sector enterprises for which it was intended, let alone for those in the social sciences.

10. Climate evaluation needs to seek more to identify the meaning of human acts. Bussis[4] has called to attention that when scientists study stars, they *do* deal with complex phenomena, but not those that mirror their thoughts: "Neither stars nor atoms construct symbolic representations of the world and then behave in accordance with their individual constructions of reality," she states. Since human acts are characterized by the meanings and intentions of the persons who perform them, the study (and evaluation) of teaching requires much more attention to clarifying the meaning of human acts.

Other Advice

Several predictions (and aspirations) identified for school climate evaluation by Daniel Stufflebeam in *A 2001 Odyssey*[5] should be added to those recommended above:

1. Evaluation methodology needs to be uniquely designed to respond to the complex and unique problems of education.

2. Evaluation methodology needs to become more sophisticated, particularly in the use of a variety of approaches, such as case studies and assessments of effects on subgroups and individuals, and in the communication of results to the various audiences.

3. Teachers, counselors, principals, and central office staff should participate in evaluations and even design and conduct their own evaluations.

4. To accomplish #3 above, a variety of training programs for different audiences needs to be developed and implemented.

Considering together the principles and Stufflebeam's recommendations causes the writer to conclude that those devising climate evaluations for the 80's will be well advised to study the progress being made at the Far West Laboratory for Educational Research and Development in researching and testing the ecological approach to the study of teaching cited earlier.

Whatever the model, climate evaluation as defined here needs to rank higher on the scale of values of educators and other stakeholders, and to receive increased resources for research, development, field testing, and implementation than has been typical in recent decades.

EVALUATING STUDENT LEARNING OUTCOMES

As a starter, assessment of student learning outcomes for the 80's requires a broader definition than that term ordinarily communicates. To *assess,* according to *Webster's Third New International Dictionary* has to do with determining "the rate or amount of," clearly implying *quantifiable* measurement. In educational circles, particularly those concerned with schooling at the elementary and secondary levels, assessment has come to be identified with the kind of evaluation reflected in the National Assessment of Educational Progress and in state assessment programs. Both of these conform to that part of the dictionary definition having to do with *amount,* since both quantify how much of a particular curriculum how many students have learned. Both national and state assessment programs are near the end of the continuum represented by the systems analysis model cited earlier.

Even narrower is the term *testing,* which is frequently applied to almost all of student evaluation. This term calls to mind for many persons in the education profession (and for most in the public) pencil-and-paper assessment, short-answer (mainly multiple-choice) tests, simple computation or cognitive recall, and normed (half those tested scored below an average) measurement. That is what standardized testing started out as more than 60 years ago and, for the most part, what it continues to be in 1980.

The way we label things frequently says much about how we conceive them, think about them, and respond to them. If the term *assessment* continues to be dominant, it will likely be thought of in terms of things to be *counted* and *rated.* And *counting* and *rating* will be the major criteria for determining student learning progress. If the term *testing* continues to be used, it will contribute to perpetuating norm-referenced, standardized tests for the preponderance of evaluation purposes.

Neither of these will serve the needs of the 80's. It is, therefore, recommended that the terms *assessment* and *testing* be replaced by *evaluation,* and that, as a qualifier of this term, *student learning progress* be used to distinguish it from the evaluation of *program* and *process* discussed in the first part of this essay.

Purposes

Exhortations on what the nature of the evaluation of student learning progress should be for the 80's will be meaningful only if the purpose of such evaluation is clear. The positions to be put forth here are based on the premise that the major purpose of evaluation is to improve instruction, which by extrapolation will, in turn, improve learning—however learning is defined.

Learning, for the purposes of this essay, is defined as the broadest possible range of knowledge, skills, attitudes, and behaviors contained in all those goals of schooling that have been identified, articulated, and agreed on for particular communities. They include skills in language arts (as broad as that term is sometimes defined to include reading, writing, speaking, listening, and forms of nonverbal communication); mathematics skills; knowledge of the cultural heritage (the social studies broadly conceived); vocational competencies; interpersonal and citizenship behaviors; self-concept; and whatever other goals are selected for schooling, be they education about consumer affairs, health, safety, sex, drug use, and myriad of other topics.

Equally important, the definition of learning in this context takes into account the person *in the process.* Thus, the definition reflects the argument presented above that in the 80's increased emphasis needs to be placed on evaluating the process of the 12 or 13 years of schooling on the basis of their being full-living, wholesome, democratic, and fulfilling experiences—to a substantial degree independent of cognitive learning outcomes.

In the 80's these purposes should increasingly replace a major purpose (in some places, the sole purpose) of the past for evaluating student learning progress: to sort and classify students for decision making on which should be permitted to proceed and which held back, which should be awarded certification of completion and which denied it, which should be permitted to pursue particular educational programs or career objectives and which refused.

The Movement Away from Evaluation That Sorts and Classifies

The 60's and 70's saw considerable movement toward recognition of the pluralistic, multicultural nature of our society and establishment of policies and processes that foster egalitarian treatment for all the citizenry. One need only ponder legislation and programs for the handicapped, actions related to women and senior citizens, and many others to confirm progress at fulfilling these commitments.

But in evaluating students, progress on achieving egalitarian goals has been less than spectacular. Those involved in evaluation have been slow to accept the premises set forth in the prologue—that all students are capable of learning, of accomplishing something at a high level of proficiency, and of becoming involved in constructive, contributing, fulfilling enterprises.

So the time is past due for our society to reflect in its commitment to schooling the same pluralistic, multicultural values, opportunities, and behaviors that have begun to characterize other aspects of society. The schools should be about identifying strengths, opening doors, and providing a broad range of options and opportunities rather than sorting and classifying students in ways that limit options.

A second compelling argument for moving away from sorting and classifying has to do with the very criteria and systems by which the sorting and classifying are accomplished—mainly cognitive criteria and psychometric processes. Both are highly defective. And both are commonly manifest in the use of standardized tests, the shortcomings of which are numerous and serious:

1. The content measured by standardized tests is thin. The tests assess mainly factual and recall learning. They measure little or not at all a student's ability to analyze, synthesize, generalize, and apply generalizations to new phenomena.

2. The items in standardized tests are often ambiguous, confusing, or just plain wrong.

3. The multiple-choice formats characteristic of most standardized tests limit learning possibilities, narrow students' thinking, and adversely affect students' opportunities and inclination to write thoughtfully and creatively.

4. Placing importance on standardized tests tends to narrow the curriculum to that which is measurable and measured by the tests.

5. The statistical processes applied to standardized tests result in half the students being below average or grade level, no matter how well they do.

6. The measurement errors in most standardized tests are so large that the tests frequently do not accurately reflect what students have learned.

7. Responding inaccurately to only a few questions can change a student's score and rank significantly enough to deny him/her rewards and opportunities in disproportion to inaccurate responses.

With deficiencies as serious and pervasive as these in standardized testing, there should be demanded in the 80's broader, deeper, more accurate, and fairer means for evaluating student learning progress—means that are more relevant to accomplishing pluralistic, multicultural, and egalitarian goals of schooling.

Characteristics of Sound Evaluation

To achieve the goals articulated above, systems for evaluating student learning progress in the 80's should reflect the following characteristics:

1. They should be broader than paper-and-pencil testing; they should be based on multiple processes and instruments of a wide variety.

2. They should be designed specifically to evaluate particular and clearly particulated instructional objectives.

3. They should be closely integrated with curriculum and instruction.

4. They should provide insights into individual learning difficulties —i.e., they should be diagnostic.

5. They should provide insights on what remediation is needed in order that learning can take place—i.e., they should assist in prescription.

6. They should report on which learning objectives individual students have accomplished out of the total agreed-upon objectives.

7. They should be as free as possible of cultural, racial, and socio-economic biases.

8. They should have the capacity for identifying strengths as well as weaknesses.

9. They should promote improved instruction and learning, and be generally positive and constructive.

The above list represents both a refinement of the evaluation purposes cited earlier and a framework for establishing sound policy on evaluating student learning progress.

Criteria for Evaluation Programs and Processes

When purpose and policy are agreed upon and in place, the following criteria need to be adhered to in developing and implementing programs for evaluating student learning progress:

1. Those who administer evaluations of student learning and then use the results should be fully involved in developing programs and processes for such evaluations.

2. The purpose and proposed uses of the results of particular evaluations should be committed to writing and communicated to students, parents, and other stakeholders. (For example, will the evaluations be used for such purposes as diagnosis, remediation, admission to advanced programs, and so on?)

3. Evaluation processes and instruments should sample what was taught; therefore, curriculum should be agreed upon, clear, and explicit.

4. Evaluation processes and instruments should be developed/selected so as to be complementary.
   a. Each should evaluate some unique dimension of that being evaluated.
   b. Professional judgment based on oral and observational processes and the products of students' work should be developed to both extend and confirm paper-and-pencil instruments.
   c. Procedures should be developed for determining the interrelationships among various evaluation processes.

5. When paper-and-pencil instruments are used, a variety of formats should be employed—e.g., essay, criticism, "story" problems, single-phrase word responses, multiple-choice, true-false, cause-and-effect analysis, completion of blank statements, eliciting of examples. No one format should make up the major part of the evaluation.

6. All processes and instruments should be thoroughly field tested and corrected based on such testing before they are implemented for decision-making purposes.

As societal goals, values, and processes change, the goals for schools will need to change. And as they do, the systems and processes by which student learning progress is evaluated will also need to be altered. For the 1980's, and beyond, evaluations themselves will need to be in a continuous state of evaluation (meta-evaluation) and updating.

REFERENCES

1. A definition of *student learning* is provided on page 129.

2. House, Ernest R. "Assumptions Underlying Evaluation Models." *Educational Researcher* 7: 4–12; March 1978.

3. Dawson, Mary B.; Tikunoff, William J.; and Ward, Beatrice A. *Toward an Ecological Theory of Teaching: A Starting Point.* San Francisco: Far West Laboratory for Educational Research and Development, n.d.

4. Bussis, Anne M. "Collaboration for What." Paper delivered at the annual conference of the American Educational Research Association, 1980.

5. From a presentation by Daniel Stufflebeam at a symposium of the American Educational Research Association, March 1980.

THE POLITICALIZATION OF EDUCATION

Leadership is a function, not a position or person. Leadership is concerned with how people can be brought together to work for common ends effectively and happily. Leadership is the ability to contribute to the achievement of those ends either through ideas or through ways of working to accomplish them. Leadership, unfortunately, is often confused with command—as the contest between the Japanese commander and the British colonel demonstrated in *The Bridge on the River Kwai*. Command, however, is always concerned with power over people, while leadership is concerned with power over problems.

Ole Sand

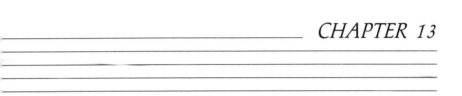

CHAPTER 13

Can Education Survive Increasing School Bureaucratization?

Roland H. Nelson

It is hardly news that schools are bureaucratic organizations. How could they be otherwise? They are public agencies, beholden to elected officials for resources, regulated by law and court decision, controlled by an administrative hierarchy, and ultimately responsible to the electorate. And what's more, schools are likely to become more bureaucratized during the 80's. The "buzz" words for such bureaucratization are already basic to the rhetoric of education: MBO, accountability, competency testing, and the like.

Does it really matter? Yes, it matters—because increasing school bureaucratization has serious implications for what teachers will be able to teach and for what students will be likely to learn.

WHAT IS BUREAUCRACY?

Bureaucracies emphasize the *logics* of organizational life. They effectively promote predictability in our workplace. Their rules, regulations, policies, and clearly defined hierarchy appeal to the need for order in us all. They are most effective when both the ends and the means are known—when what is to be done and how it is to be done are agreed upon by "reasonable" people.

Bureaucracies are less effective and often dysfunctional for managing the *dynamics* of organizational life because these dynamics are ever-changing. What is to be done (ends) and how to do it (means) are neither precise nor agreed upon because of varied situational contingencies. The rules, regulations, and policies designed for a predictable environment do not meet the reality of one that is constantly changing.

What is the typical bureaucratic response to the dynamics of organizational life? What is that response when current rules, regulations, and policies do not solve the problem at hand? Create more rules, regulations, and policies, and establish new bureaus. To the bureaucrat, what is to be done and the best way to do it can, or should, always be known. Seldom is the bureaucratic response one of the following: Let those doing the job take care of it; or suspend the rules; or decrease administrative positions—because the premise on which the *logics* of bureaucracies rests is this: Problems in the organization are primarily a function of limited individual rationality; rationality of action is achieved for the individual by organizing her or his activities through bureaucratic structure; therefore, when problems arise, they are to be solved by more rules (*guidelines* is the current euphemism), regulations, and supervision. One is reminded of the agonizing rationalization of the Grand Inquisitor:

> The most painful secrets of their conscience, all, all they will bring to us, and we shall have an answer for all. And they will be glad to believe our answer, for it will save them from the great anxiety and terrible agony they endure at present in making a free decision for themselves.[1]

But bureaucracies are not the villains of this piece. They are highly effective structures for promoting order in complex organizations. Our quarrel with them is the seductive nature of their promises because we all experience that "great anxiety" and "terrible agony" in making a free decision for ourselves. They mitigate that anxiety and assuage that agony with their promises of a rational, predictable world where what to teach, how to teach it well, and to whom to teach it are fully known and prescribed.

No, bureaucracies are not the villains. We recognize that complex societies require complex organizations, that all of us will need to be members of complex organizations so long as we desire the benefits of a complex society. We want our pension plans, our guaranteed salaries, our reasonably predictable work environments. We want those things that require the coordination of the many and varied efforts of experts of myriad degree and kind. Bureaucracy provides us that coordination. It provides the logics of organizational life: (1) statements of goals, objectives, and purposes; (2) policies, rules, and regulations prescribing who will do what, when, and how; (3) differentiated task assignments promoting individual specialization—i.e., teachers, counselors, aides, librarians; and (4) an hierarchy of management to coordinate the diverse functions performed by the specialists and to interface with the hierarchy of other complex organizations such as government agencies, legislatures, and professional associations.

The strength of bureaucracy lies in its ability to lend structure to human activity, and therein also lies its greatest limitation—it is the nature of the bureaucrat to structure when it is neither necessary nor appropriate. The bureaucrat is at her or his best in stable (static), predictable situations. She or he is at her or his worst in dynamic or rapidly changing situations.

As schools become more bureaucratized, they increasingly stress uniformity of both practice and results. Students are categorized and labeled. Once labeled, special programs are established for them, specialists are trained to direct the special programs, and more administrators are added to coordinate the activities of the specialists. So much specialization and coordination are beyond the ken of the poor teacher whose role becomes that of bureaucratic functionary. The student is provided instruction according to her or his organizational prototype, and success is now defined by how well she or he meets the standards of that prototype. S/he is not an individual—s/he is a statistic.

It is also a characteristic of bureaucracies to take on more and more tasks because each new task creates the need for new specializations and promotes organizational growth. (A primary measure of success for the bureaucrat is how many people report to her or him.) Thus, bureaucrats try to convince the public that they can solve more and more of the public's problems, as if there were no real limit to what any one organization can do. But no agency should undertake what is impossible to accomplish, and much of what schools now claim to be able to do is probably administratively impossible. The decision makers, the bureaucrats atop the hierarchy, are not likely to know, much less admit, that any task is too difficult to perform because their reality increasingly becomes the reality of the bureaucratic self-fulfilling prophecy: Once a program is mandated, it exists; rules and regulations define its existence; data are produced verifying its existence. For example, exceptional children are to be integrated into the regular classroom; resources are provided; regulations are promulgated that mandate *mainstreaming.* Reports filter back up the hierarchy that mainstreaming is being done to meet mandated criteria; therefore, the logic goes, mainstreaming is a success —exceptional children are integrated into the regular classroom. Orwell in his novel *1984* described such "logic" as "double think, a vast system of mental cheating." He wrote that, "In our society, those who have the best knowledge [the most data] of what is happening are also those who are furtherest from seeing the world as it is."[2]

THE DILEMMA

How do we manage the dilemma of preserving the merits of bureaucracy that maintain and promote the logics of the organization and that still ensure the freedom of individuals to deal effectively with the dynamics of the organization? How do we maintain the strengths of bureaucracy—mustering and accounting for vast resources, coordinating the efforts of varied specialists and experts, and providing a "predictable" work environment? How do we do that and, at the same time, enhance the abilities of the organization's people to do uncommon things in uncommon situations, to be unpredictably predictable and predictably unpredictable—in short, to be creative in an organization designed to promote uniformity?

RESPONSES TO MANAGING THE DILEMMA

I suggest that a number of responses are likely to occur in this decade as a result of the increasing bureaucratization of schools. Each has distinct advantages and limitations; some are more likely to win acceptance than others; some are more likely to improve education for students than others; none offers the panacea their proponents will claim for them.

I shall discuss five of those responses, citing some of their advantages and limitations and their likelihood of acceptance.

The Traditional Bureaucratic Response

The traditional bureaucratic response is likely to be a prevalent response during the 80's. Since bureaucratic management responds to educational problems and demands through increased standardization, this decade will see an increase in standardized tests (current legal questions notwithstanding), standardized curriculums, and teacher-proof instructional materials. Additional pressures for standardization will come from categorical legislation, the accountability movement, and court decisions mandating standardized educational results.

Though the traditional bureaucratic response promises organizational growth, it is likely to effect little improvement in what goes on in the classroom. Though more data will be produced for decision makers—i.e., legislators, administrators, and study committees—the data will come to the decision makers filtered, categorized, and prototyped; phantom students, taught phantom subjects, by phantom teachers. What is really going on in the classroom will be quite different from what those at the top believe is going on, but their data and techniques for analyzing it will ensure that they never find out.

The Counterbureaucratic Response

The counterbureaucratic response will increase during the 80's as a reaction to the increase of the traditional bureaucratic response. The counterbureaucratic response is a legalistic and adversarial response that seeks to establish a counterforce identical in form and power to the traditional bureaucracy that it wishes to control and/or neutralize.

The counterbureaucracy is composed of those with little individual power within the traditional bureaucracy—i.e., teachers—but who collectively, through their professional associations, can exercise power with the political decision makers and the public at large. The counterbureaucracy collects its data, structures its reality, and hopes to confront with equal force the traditional bureaucracy in legally prescribed negotiations, political power plays, and formal campaigns for public support.

Unfortunately, the counterbureaucracy is primarily reactive, not pro-active. It reacts to the strategy and tactics of the traditional bureaucracy rather than promoting strategies and tactics of its own. It reacts to increased testing, teacher-proof materials, and accountability by pointing up their shortcomings, but it proposes as options other forms of bureaucratic control substituting teachers for administrators as the controllers.

The primary advantages of the counterbureaucratic response are these: It neutralizes much of the power of the traditional bureaucracy, and it provides the adversarial responses of a "loyal" opposition. Thus, the public and its decision makers are assured that educational issues will be debated. Its primary disadvantage, however, is that it reinforces what the traditional bureaucracy has wrought: widespread belief among the "little people" that they are anonymous folk in a mass society, members of an organization whose reality they can only know through the eyes of those at the top. What seems real to the anonymous folk must not be real at all. They no longer can trust their senses. What they see and hear, they dare not believe.

The Reformer Response

The reformer response will be espoused frequently during the 80's, but its success will be limited for at least two reasons: Its advocates will be primarily academicians from the world of the university whose credibility with those on the "firing line" is already diminishing; their proposals, though attractive in the abstract, seem to suffer grievously when implemented in the world of the schools.

The reformers will come bearing various labels—i.e., humanistic education, moral education, basic education—all promising reform in the name of an abstract good. Each holds some promise for school improvement—but only if viewed as curriculum options and not as means of school reform.

The reformers believe and will endeavor to convince that they should be the "new kings." Though they will renounce the bureaucracy, they will try to gain control of it because their means to reform require the complex mechanisms of bureaucratic control. They would add, however, a subtle but highly significant control strategy. Recognizing the limitations of rules and regulations for prescribing human behavior in complex organizations, they would emphasize the need for *elan, esprit,* a *sense of community* to promote a psychological dependency on the organization by its members. (Rules and regulations would be superfluous if people would naturally do the "right" thing.) Their argument for such control is this: (1) Individual "good" is a function of promoting the "abstract good" or orthodoxy (individual "good" is not defined); (2) School organizations now promote that "abstract good" or orthodoxy; (3) Therefore, individuals who do not support the organization are, in fact, not doing what is "good" for them and are not "well." Since these individuals are "ill," they should not be punished by invoking rules and regulations; rather, they should be helped to become "well" again by their peers and their hierarchical superiors. To be "well" is to cooperate fully with the organization.

The reformers might make substantive contributions to education in the 80's if they can accept their role as technical advisors to educational leaders. However, they probably cannot because they view themselves as leaders of reform, though without portfolio, and, thus, cannot be content with modest proposals for school improvement. In striving for the whole cake they may well lose their slice.

The Romanticist Response

The romanticist response for the 80's will advocate a return to a simpler time and place. Its advocates view the complexities of educational organization as the real enemy. They believe that education is not complex but that the institutions designed to educate make it so.

The romanticist response is simplistic, and, as is often the case with simple solutions, it has its appeal. Some romanticists would "de-school" society. Since schools aren't doing their job, do away with them and return to a simpler (primitive?) way to educate. Other romanticists would do away with the complexity of schools through voucher plans requiring students and schools to fend for themselves in the marketplace. Another group would decentralize, debureaucratize, and return to the small, local school districts of a century ago.

The romanticists will probably not become a significant force in effecting any real change unless they are able to unify the many divergent groups currently unhappy with public schools—e.g., segregationists, educational elitists, religious fundamentalists, and taxpayer unions. But the romanticists are persistent because their vision has universal appeal to our yearning for simpler times. As schools become more bureaucratized, assuming more and more tasks, many of us may wish to throw up our hands and say "away with the mess." Such a response would be dangerously naive. It makes no more sense than a return to local militia for defense, a return to the family market for our food, a return to the locally owned utility for our power. I must say, however, as I dismiss the romanticists as a major force in the 80's, that I do so with a real twinge of nostalgia.

The Realistic Response

The realistic response to increasing school bureaucratization is designed to manage the *natural tension* between the logics and dynamics of school organizations. It would maintain the bureaucratic structure but, at the same time, limit its growth in two significant ways: (1) by defining more rigorously those problems that schools can deal with effectively, and (2) by allocating more resources directly to those in daily contact with students.

The realistic response requires the courage to admit that no one organization, no matter how dedicated its members, can do all things well for all. Its proponents would ask such questions as these: What do schools do well now? What do they not do very well? What do they do very poorly? The realistics are concerned with determining "what is" before moving to "what can be" or "what ought to be." They question the ability of schools to deal with such problems as drugs, pathological antisocial behavior, and standardized learning results for students of varied interests and aptitude.

The realistics would say, "Let us take stock of what individual teachers can effectively do, the *dynamics* of the classroom, lest we fall victim to the bureaucratic *logics* that all things are possible through the proper structuring of human activity."

The realistics assume that what schools do well is dependent upon what teachers, and others in frequent contact with students, do for them. Thus, their response emphasizes allocating resources directly to those in daily contact with students. If, for example, a new task is to be taken on by the teacher, is class size to be significantly reduced? Will the budget for individual teaching materials be significantly increased? Will specialists be available to each teacher to work with students (not to work with teachers to tell them how to work with students)? Will in-service education, meaningful to and requested by the teacher, be provided? With increasing job demands and, in turn, job complexity, will the teacher be "managed" less by rules, regulations, and bureaucratic superordinates?

The realistic response confronts the traditional bureaucratic assumption that as the teacher's work becomes more complex, the teacher's performance needs to be more carefully prescribed. The realistics contend that as the job becomes more complex, bureaucratic structure should increasingly serve rather than prescribe for the teacher.

The realistic approach could be a salutary alternative to the increasing bureaucratization of schools. Its impact will be limited, however, because it contravenes too many current shibboleths: for example, that schools can do more and more, better and better; that the means to do more and more lie in more personnel specialization; that standardized results mean equality of educational opportunity. Further, it questions the bureaucratic imperative that the dynamics of the organization are best managed by making them predictable and, thus, synonymous with the organization's logics; in other words, what goes on in the classroom improves as it is more closely controlled.

THE PROFESSIONAL AND THE BUREAUCRACY: A PARADOX

The five responses to school bureaucratization address the following question: How can we organize more efficiently to educate students? All five responses assume that education will improve with increased organizational efficiency. That assumption ignores, however, the paradox endemic to bureaucracies that employ professionals. The professional is employed to meet the challenge of the organization's dynamics, to minister to individual student needs in idiosyncratic and even unique ways; but the professional is expected to do so within the logics of the bureaucracy that mandates prototype instruction for prototype students.

How can we develop, encourage, and nurture individual professionals who can effectively cope with the bureaucratic paradox, who can cooperate with the bureaucracy but not be co-opted by it? How can we make certain that such professionals maintain their professional integrity and their ability to practice as professionals in the face of all manner of pressure to become bureaucratic functionaries?

We can strengthen the professionals' abilities to make and implement individual decisions. We can encourage the professionals to "manage" the bureaucracy rather than be managed by it. We can remember that bureaucracies provide effectively for the diverse needs of students only when professionals in daily contact with students decide what to do in the classroom. We can then evaluate proposals for school organization according to how much they strengthen the profession of teaching.

REFERENCES

1. Dostoyevsky, Fyodor. *The Brothers Karamazov.* (Translated by Constance Garnett.) New York: The Modern Library, 1950. p. 269.

2. Orwell, George. *1984.* New York: Harcourt Brace, 1949. p. 95.

CHAPTER 14

The Role of Citizen Participation in the Schools

Dorothy V. Meyer

Although the ballot box is the symbol of participatory democracy, many persons are no longer satisfied with simply voting: They want to become involved. This is particularly true when the issue is the function of the public schools. The local school board, duly elected or appointed to represent the people, often appears distant and unresponsive. People intuitively recognize that the organizational arrangements of a school board make it virtually impossible for the members both to oversee the schools and to remain sensitive to the concerns of the community. Yet of all social institutions, people feel closest to the schools. They went to school, their children go to school, and the same can be said of their neighbors and friends. People want to be involved with the schools— not so much because they want to participate in government but because they want to be involved with the schools themselves.

For years the "Home and School" or "Parent and Teacher" arrangement was viewed as an adequate model for citizen participation in the schools. By design, such organizations encouraged the parents of school children and no one else in the community to work in cooperation with a school staff. The focus of such arrangements tended to be narrow in scope, concerned with tangential issues, and, in the main, supportive of the school program. In the past parent groups appeared to function best in a variety of middle-class settings. Such groups provided "room mothers" (a kind of parent paraprofessional for the elementary school classroom), chaperones for the yearly field trip, and a variety of baked goods for the Spring Bazaar, the profits from which provided the "frills" that had not been included in the budget prepared by the central administration.

Formal meetings held by such organizations were often more social than informative. Following a brief business agenda, occasions such as the arts and crafts exhibit, the brass ensemble concert, and the gymnastic performance usually highlighted the evening. The most well-attended function was the annual "go to school" night, a guided tour behind the chalk curtain. Parents trekked along well-polished corridors, past impressive displays in wall cabinets, into classrooms whose walls and desks displayed only the "perfect papers." The rooms were so clean and antiseptic that the usual daily occupants would hardly recognize them. To be sure, this scene in middle-class neighborhoods is far more inviting than what occurred or did not occur in many lower socioeconomic neighborhoods, but it hardly provided meaningful participation in the function of the schools.

On the surface, at least, such arrangements have appeared to be supportive of the traditional function of the schools. Seldom do parents in suburbia muster mass support or protest efforts over school issues since they know the strategies for constraining the schools to meet the needs of their individual children. They tend not to follow the formalities of moving through the maze of the bureaucratic organization, exhausting all efforts at each level. They make their concerns known to those holding positions in the upper level of the organizational table, not because of a strong distaste for the slow bureaucratic process but because they are acquainted with the bureaucratic actors in the upper echelon of the organization through social clubs, business organizations, or places of neighborhood residence. With satisfaction usually attained by this procedure, participation in mass efforts would be deemed not only unsuitable and inappropriate but unnecessary as well.

Poor people, through experience, have not found it possible to penetrate school bureaucratic organizations, and they have judged that the schools were not providing for the needs of their children. In making their demands upon the system, they have tended to approach those individuals who, to them, represented the schools. Inevitably they sought out those whose positions were on the lower level of the bureaucratic structure, those who were most constrained by the rules of the organization. When results were not forthcoming, they viewed the schools as unresponsive, and they saw themselves as not being represented in the educational process of their children. As individuals they could not effect change; other means needed to be found.

During several significant periods in the 1960's and 1970's, participation by citizens who have been traditionally excluded from the decision-making process emerged. The mechanism for participation was initiated not by locally elected officials or professionals, nor even by the people themselves, but by the federal government in response to growing unrest in urban areas. Several significant pieces of legislation were enacted, and accompanying guidelines mandated the involvement of the persons to be served.[1] The Community Action Program, Model Cities, and Title I of the Elementary and Secondary Education Act (ESEA) called for a level of citizen participation far beyond that which had previously been established.

As part of our nation's war on poverty, more than a thousand Community Action Programs were authorized in the Economic Opportunity Act of 1964 which mandated "maximum feasible participation." This call was inclusive. Not only were school boards, human services agencies, and political, business, labor, and religious leaders to participate but also the citizens of the poor neighborhoods. The programs developed were as diverse as the people participating in the planning. All programs were designed to provide needed health care, social services, education, housing, municipal services, and the like for persons in a designated, blighted geographic area.

Emphasis in the Model Cities program, funded under the Demonstration Cities and Metropolitan Development Act of 1966, was on the need to serve the poor and disadvantaged living in the neglected areas. "Widespread citizen participation" was mandated in order to include the residents of the areas to be served. Model Cities legislation intended that the program would benefit neighborhoods that had not been well served by local government.

Schools were also included in the new focus on citizen participation. Although Title I of the ESEA of 1965 (a response to the special needs of schools with a significant percentage of pupils from low-income families) did not initially include input from the local level, over time directives were given that called for organizational arrangements that would establish local advisory committees. Three years after the program was initiated, the regulations were revised to require "maximum practical involvement" of the parents of the children in the programs. Even though the amount and kind of participation of the parents fluctuated greatly from city to city, the government mandate was geared toward increasing the level of parent participation.

In all of these programs, lower-income people, acting collectively, were able to make gains, however modest, that they had been unable to make individually. Some of these programs are gone now and others are severely curtailed, but those who were participants learned how to make themselves heard. It is doubtful that programs will ever be designed again without including those to be served.

Citizen participation has taken many forms in the past two decades, but the massive protest efforts of those yearning to be heard are the ones we can vividly call to mind. Civil rights marches, student antiwar rallies, antischool-busing protests, and the bitter struggle for community control of the Ocean Hill-Brownsville schools in New York City—all serve to point out that individuals who had no clout in the marketplace could be heard if they acted collectively. In this way the disaffected entered the decision-making process.

Recently I read an article addressed to educators on the subject of community participation that implied that advisory councils in school systems were here to stay. And since this was so, we must choose the membership of such councils carefully. Furthermore, if we, the educators, organized the councils well, the article continued, they would not make poor decisions. The implication seemed to be not that the members of the council should be chosen as representative of the district but rather that they should be chosen for their past support of us. In other words, avoid anyone who might make trouble. The tone of the article also implied that the council should function solely in an advisory capacity, neither formulating policy nor engaging in any decision-making process. Fortunately, the segment of the public that must rely so heavily on the schools in order for their youngsters to have a chance to move ahead has long since abandoned participation in this kind of scheme. Even residents of middle-class neighborhoods who participated in meetings that were characterized as quiet, polite, and manageable are no longer content with merely an advisory role.

As we look toward future models of citizen participation, it may be useful to use a schema to describe ways in which people become involved. Sherry Arnstein[2] cites eight rungs on the ladder of participation. These levels of involvement extend from the lowest rung, which she designates as manipulation, up through degrees of tokenism to delegated power and citizen control. While the ladder may be viewed as a useful simplification, it illustrates the issue so many have missed—that there are significant gradations of citizen participation. In enlarging the participatory role of the public in the 80's there is much to be learned from what worked and what did not in programs previously undertaken. In a new decade characterized as a time of uncertainty, it is well to examine anew and consider direction for the participatory role of citizens in public education. Times of turmoil such as we witnessed in the 60's and 70's are often followed by periods of relative acquiescence. Although we are in such a period now, it would be wise not to slacken our efforts to involve the citizens in the decision-making process of public education.

Who are these citizens who should participate? Public involvement in the affairs of the schools has in the past been almost exclusively the purview of those with school-age children. Yet, two-thirds of our adult population do not have children in the schools, but do have a stake in the kinds of citizens our schools produce. Efforts should be undertaken to include a much larger segment of the local population than is presently involved. If participation is extended only to the "parent group," then we will have succeeded only in adding to the decision-making process one more segment of society that does not totally represent the community, an achievement we wish not to make. As broad a representation as possible should be the aim of those who encourage involvement from citizens in the school district. By their organizational structure and manageable size, area school districts can accommodate community participation. Even big city school systems have been decentralized so that a cogent, identifiable district exists at the local level.

How should citizens participate? It is here that leaders in each school district must use their most imaginative thoughts lest they add one more level to an already complex bureaucratic structure and then witness citizens organizations that become nonfunctional in some facet of the bureaucratic scheme.

The bureaucratic structure of the school system that has over time been able to deflect every intrusion must now in good faith redesign its organization in order to bring representative groups of citizens into a meaningful level of participation. Citizens committees, either elected or appointed but preferably elected, should function along with the professionals at significant stages in the structure. A mere advisory role will not do. If community organizations have not before had meaningful input into the school's decision-making process, then perhaps they might begin in an advisory capacity, but they should remain at that level of participation only briefly; people only participate if they believe their contribution makes a difference.

Ideally, citizens along with school personnel should work toward having such committees invested with delegated power. This, of course, will take planning. At this level in the Arnstein schema, negotiations between citizens and professionals can result in citizens' achieving decision-making authority in a particular plan or program. Such power was achieved by several citizen boards in federally funded neighborhood programs during the 70's. A study of their successes and failures in the decision-making role may serve to help design a viable participatory model for the schools of the 80's.

No matter how carefully a mechanism is designed to include all segments of the community in the decision-making process, there will be those who prefer not to participate in a planned organization but who will from time to time demand to be heard in the marketplace. This is another legitimate means of participation. This kind of involvement is often precipitated when opportunity for significant participation through institutionalized arrangements such as various kinds of established citizens committees appears to have been stifled or coopted by the larger bureaucratic organization. The concerns of those who choose this method of participation must not go unheeded. Likewise, caution must be exercised in considering the issues lest the method evoked for presentation be more powerful than the concern expressed.

When single-interest citizens organizations make demands of the public school system, policymakers and their administrative staffs must discern for whom these groups speak and how accurately they reflect the views of their constituents. Caution should be exercised to assure that their constituency is a viable group within the school district. Special interest groups have been known to play out their scenarios in selected communities after soliciting the support of only a very few persons.

Likewise, problems may emerge when self-appointed persons, speaking for a much smaller segment of the community than they care to admit, push for special interests. Care must be taken that one segment of interest is not pursued at the expense of another.

Some organizations, in order to win support for their cause, play on the emotions of citizens regarding seemingly volatile issues. Such groups often succeed in packing public meetings with large numbers of boisterous persons whose shrill voices bent with emotion create a climate in which facts become blurred and an opportunity for a reasonable discussion of the issues is lost.

On occasion there will be those who demand that action be taken for today and that we worry about tomorrow when it comes. While immediate solutions may satisfy short-range needs, they could have far-reaching consequences and serve to cripple long-range educational plans.

The elitists, who may be heard singly or through organized efforts, may use their influence because of their positions of social or economic importance in the community. Because of their positions, their rhetoric, at least on the surface, appears convincing.

Each one of these may well have a very legitimate concern or issue to bring before the board. The issue, if enacted, may serve the community well, but on the other hand it may not.[3] A concern posed by this kind of participation is the potential that it offers for overzealous responses to their demands by the representatives of the local school system.

What should be the agenda for participation? Marilyn Gittell[4] suggests that there are four areas of involvement critical to full participation by the community: (1) curriculum, (2) personnel, (3) pupil policy, and (4) budget. Let us look briefly at what this may imply.

Curriculum

From our country's inception, we have rejected the concept of the "one best system" of education nationally; yet, we have tolerated such arrangements locally. How many times have we seen one teaching method instituted systemwide? Thousands of us today barely have a legible handwriting because we were victims of a school system's commitment to the notion that there was one best method of teaching children to write.

How often have we witnessed the adoption of one social studies textbook systemwide, thus depriving the young of divergent points of view?

How often have we seen the learning process geared to somebody else's time? How frequently have students been busily involved in solving an algebraic equation only to have the sound of a bell signal the need to stop immediately, gather one's books, hurry along a hallway, walk up two flights of stairs, proceed down another hallway, and enter a classroom just in time to conjugate verbs in French.

As educators we need to provide educational programs of choice in every school. No longer will all fourth grades in one building be similar. One classroom may be progressive, while another may be traditional and yet another somewhere in between. Something for everyone. Parents would choose programs best suited to their children's needs. To provide for individual differences, a traditional classroom may be chosen for one child and a progressive classroom for another child in the same family. Teachers will have choices, too. Who among us has not yearned to structure a class quite differently from the prescribed manner acceptable in the schools to which we were assigned?

Personnel

A decade ago we were still moving at an almost frantic pace in our effort to cope with the ever increasing school population, only to have the situation reverse itself in the 80's. Today, rapidly declining enrollments have not only curtailed the number of new candidates seeking employment in education but also severely truncated the careers of those already so engaged. While opportunities for employment appear rather dismal, some educators possessing skills unavailable within the staff in certain school districts, albeit few in number, are being sought for positions. Likewise, present school staff are selected for other positions within the system. With sufficient opportunity for planning, no longer must positions be filled by nightfall, lest the sun rise on a curriculum center without a coordinator or a classroom without a teacher.

A well-planned selection process for filling positions should provide not only for participation from the educational staff but also for strong input from the community representatives. A virtual partnership should emerge from such a process. By statute, the final authority for hiring personnel rests with the school board, but whatever determination it makes should reflect the desires of those who participated in the process of screening candidates for consideration.

Pupil Policy

The burden of establishing new acceptable codes of behavior for the young appears to have been placed squarely upon the shoulders of those who are responsible for the operation of the schools, and more specifically on those closest to the youngsters—the classroom teachers. The role of the teachers has become much more difficult in this time when societal norms have undergone rapid change. Every effort should be undertaken to have representatives from both the community and the school work together in establishing acceptable pupil policies. In the past, scattershot methods of handling nearly explosive situations have only served to exacerbate conditions. Schools as social institutions reflect the community at large. In periods of change, we can avoid the turbulence that often accompanies such times by together—community and schools—addressing issues that have hitherto caused difficulty and dissension. By supporting one another we can establish some common policies rather than being perceived as working at cross purposes. Attaining this will not be easy.

Budget

Although sources of school revenue vary widely from state to state, with few major exceptions a sizeable percentage of the costs for educating the young is derived from monies appropriated at the local level. Strong interest in school budgers is generated when citizens realize that the major portion of their property tax dollar is used for this purpose. As with everything else in times of inflation, school costs are escalating rapidly with no relief in sight. Declining enrollments will not indicate a reduction in costs but will reveal an increase in per pupil expenditures. Hopefully we will not witness again the several situations where public schools were forced to close for significant periods of time due to lack of funds. Persons who are knowledgeable of their schools and active in a participatory manner can be strong supporters in helping school people receive and maintain an adequate budget. Citizens must be in at the ground level in budget preparation sessions. It is unfair to seek their participation when the budget planning process is so far advanced that they are asked only to give rubber stamp approval.

It is well and good to advocate a participatory role in the governance of schools by those in the community regardless of age, sex, marital status, and the like. It is well that this role be more than merely involvement so that decision making can take place. But responsible decisions cannot be made in a vacuum. Meaningful decisions can be made only when decision makers have access to adequate information. Professionals in some fields have been known for their unwillingness to provide even the most basic information to those whom they serve. Although educators have not been so characterized, at times the information they have provided for the public has been less than adequate to permit any significant contribution from the citizens. Let it not be said of educators, as it often has been said of other professionals, that they maintain control by controlling information. Information is power, and, without it, participants remain powerless.

In addition to providing adequate information, educators must provide a climate in which citizen participation can function effectively. Unfortunately, the realities of many school organizations can continue to set sharp limitations on what local efforts by citizens can accomplish. This should not be so.

Development of strong citizen participation is possible because of the local nature of our nation's school system. Even so, participation can be viewed as difficult and often highly complex. School people, uneasy lest a wrong decision be made, may view citizen participation as a risky endeavor. Others may perceive it as useful only in times of crisis. Active participation is difficult to sustain, but we cannot operate schools solely in crisis situations. Whatever the risks, whatever the efforts needed to maintain participation, bringing the community into full participation in the decision-making process can serve only to strengthen the role of our schools.

REFERENCES

1. Many theories abound, and there is a vast proliferation of material by a number of social scientists writing on the urban scene as to why such participation became a part of the several programs. Most viewed it as political—a means of counteracting protest movements. The intent of this essay is not to present another theory for the inclusion of participation in the legislation and guidelines of the programs, but rather to reflect on what can be learned from such participation and to make suggestions for ways citizens can have participatory roles in the public schools.

2. Arnstein, Sherry R. "Eight Rungs on the Ladder of Citizen Participation." *Citizen Participation: Effecting Community Change.* (Edited by Edgar S. Cahn and Barry A. Passett.) New York: Praeger Publishers, 1971. pp. 69–91.

3. For a more detailed discussion of the kinds of problems that surface in public participation in a noneducational project, see: Cupps, D. Stephen. "Emerging Problems of Citizen Participation." *Public Administration Review* 37: 478–487; October 1977.

4. Gittell, Marilyn. "Community Control of Education." *The Politics of Urban Education.* (Edited by Marilyn Gittell and Alan G. Hevesi.) New York: Praeger Publishers, 1969. p. 364.

_____ CHAPTER 15

_____

_____

_____

_____

Closed Captive Bureaucracies
Elizabeth C. Wilson

Are school systems closed captive bureaucracies? Of course they are. Rhetorical questions expect simple answers and hope, by the impertinence of the question, to seal off further discussion and investigation. In this case, however, our dander is up. Let's insist upon some description of the phenomenon and at least a nod toward an explanation of how it developed and what can be done about it.

First of all, how do we know that school systems are closed captive bureaucracies? Partially by living in and with schools and school systems and listening to the kinds of complaints that surface within the inner sanctums, and partially by attending to the media and reading the local press. Some school troubles have hit even the funny papers. One does not have to look very far to document the charge.

Parents grumble that they get better replies from the copying machine or from the computer spewing out test scores than they do from principals and from central office administrators. As a consequence, energetic parents, having learned that the squeaky wheel gets attention, quite frequently organize lobby groups and press for hearings and concessions from boards of education. Principals are snowed by paper work emanating from the central office and have little or no time to tend to instruction. Teachers are run ragged keeping the undisciplined in line and tending to social ills like desecration of public property and drug and child abuse rather than to traditional teaching demands. They respond by barricading themselves in their classrooms, by becoming shrill, militant leaders of their respective teacher organizations, or by informing the press of their plight. For example, one finds the following lament in the *Washington Post:*

> . . . the real reason I am at home is that I could not face another demoralizing day of matching wits with a bunch of insolent and insubordinate 14-year-olds who have never been taught it is not proper to swear at, interrupt or otherwise mock and insult a teacher. . . .
>
> I was exhausted, burned out and frustrated from the effort necessary to enforce a minimum of classroom order so that the few kids interested in learning might have a fair chance.
>
> Too many people would blame the conduct of the students and their declining sum of knowledge . . . solely on the educational laxity of the late '60s and '70s. But what is most frightening about today's classroom goes well beyond the established lack of students' demonstrable skills. . . . There is a violence and a lack of personal control that characterizes the way students relate to each other and, more noticeably, to those in authority. . . .
>
> The old alliance between school, church and home has run amok. . . .[1]

Students, especially those in large high schools, get depressed and despondent about lack of warmth and personal attention on the part of adults in the school setting, and they lean even more heavily upon their peers for support and for fixing standards of behavior.

Individuals find it almost impossible to be heard in the ordinary course of affairs. A crisis seems to be necessary to get the attention of school system officials.

So what has happened to the school system bureaucracy and governing body? Theoretically they are supposed to provide services and supervision to the series of schools within their jurisdiction. They were designed to take care of inequities in matters like cost per pupil and the quality of the teaching staff in schools representing different mixes of socioeconomic backgrounds, to bring expensive and scarce services to the schools, and to streamline the administrative activities common to all schools that can be handled more efficiently and cheaply on a large-scale basis than by a single school. Yet, the people who attend to these tasks at the central office levels of school systems are as discouraged as those who work in local schools. Both the professional staff and the members of boards of education mutter that they have little or no control over what goes on in the schools.

How did this situation develop? Let's start trying to answer that question by making some very mundane observations about school systems. Let's note, first of all, that *a school system* is more than a single school with its students, teachers, parents, principal, support personnel, and the community it serves, although school systems must deal with each of these groups of people directly or indirectly. A school system by definition consists of more than one school. There are often many schools and many levels of schools within a school system—schools that are governed by a board of education and by a superintendent of schools who usually serves as the executive secretary for the board and as the immediate supervisor of the auxiliary services provided by the school system. The school board is the duly constituted legal body immediately responsible for the quality of education provided by any given district. If school districts are very large, there can be another layer of administration between the central office and the schools.

Another common situation worthy of mention is the fact that school systems do not operate by themselves with respect to governance. They are officially responsible to state education authorities and to state legislatures. For example, the state makes demands on local school systems by means of state-mandated standards and laws that stipulate such particulars as the number of days schools must be open, curriculum requirements, and teacher qualifications. The state also holds powerful purse strings which it can withhold in cases of noncompliance.

Looming over all the states and local school systems are the FEDs. Local school systems are increasingly governed by federal law. The most far-reaching example in recent years has been the Supreme Court decision relating to desegregation of the schools. But Congress also has a powerful voice. The Education for All Handicapped Children Act, new rules relating to Indo-Chinese refugees, and regulations concerning the sale of "junk" foods are all examples of the range of local school activity in which the Congress and the executive branch of the federal government are involved. The government of local school systems definitely wears a layered look in this day and age. The notion that our school systems enjoy local autonomy is a myth.

The myth of local autonomy for school systems is underscored by the fact that they suffer from the same disease that infects governing bodies of all kinds and at all levels today. This disease, rampant since the era of the 60's, is called *government by vocal militant constituencies*—i.e.,

158

pressure groups or lobbies. In other words, school systems like other public bodies are now practically ungovernable. They are squeezed from the top, from the bottom, and from all sides. They spend most of their time trying to appease militant constituencies, or making the internal arrangements needed to accommodate another new regulation or program mandated from above, such as health screening or new programs for the handicapped (to be managed without funding), or supervising the human rights issues being underlined by ethnic minorities and other underdeveloped populations like women or the poor. Very seldom do they find the time to look closely at curriculum and instruction. Indeed, the school is fast becoming society's major agent for delivery of social welfare services as well as for picking up the pieces of the disintegration of the family as an institution.

Each of these laudable health and social welfare programs adds another task to those traditionally associated with the schools. And each requires its own set of specialists, supervisory staff, and compulsory reports at all levels. As a consequence, the governing body of the school system is bogged down in paper work. Much of this gets passed down to the local school. When teachers and principals complain about increasing numbers of reports and increasing amounts of time devoted to managerial and administrative duties rather than to teaching and to educational leadership, they are right. Three or four years ago a bitter junior high school principal counted 435 different communications received from his school system supervisors within the space of two months. The situation is undoubtedly worse now.

And so, instead of all systems within the school system being GO, all systems are clogged, not only with regulations and mandatory new programs but also with political noises of many kinds. Since the brave new world of the 60's, when many special groups learned to shout loudly and to turn the political screws, governing bodies have been immobilized by the need to attend to and to mollify vocal pressure groups of one sort or another. They not only load down the system with static, but also they often infiltrate the system. Quite frequently, for example, each school board member has a special interest group that is her or his particular concern and to whom she/he is politically indebted. Cagey staff members learn to play this game as well, resulting in either empire-building at the expense of the whole school system or stagnation of action because consensus cannot be reached within the school board. Hardly anyone really pays attention to the needs of the school system as a whole. The glue that once held the system together has become unstuck.

Another insidious result of the politicizing of separate constituencies within the system is its effects upon school system professionals—middle and top management personnel. The unsticking of the glue breeds internal as well as external power grabs. The internal game within the "educational leader" group, particularly in larger systems, becomes who can win friends and influence people within the power structure rather than who can help to improve the quality of education for young people. Rewards go to the glib and to those who have established a successful image within the power structure. In-fighting becomes a way of life and a major demand on the psychic energy of the system.

Power is also the name of the game for teachers associations or unions. They have learned over the last two decades how to negotiate for wages and "perks." More recently they have added the considerable power of the teacher vote to their list of accomplishments. They are now able to "deliver" a vote at local, state, and national levels. Efforts to upgrade the profession through such means as improvement of the curriculum or enhancement of the quality of teaching used to rank high among the activities of these organizations. Such efforts have gradually moved lower and lower on the scale of priorities within the organized profession.

Put all these elements together and the whole at the school system level is both ugly and unmanageable. More and more well-qualified and dedicated people are opting out of leadership roles in the profession, especially those of superintendent and high school principal. Sophisticated top management people and school board members frantically make abortive efforts to break the log jam by relying more and more on such technological tools as management by objectives, programmed budgets, computer printouts, and Skinnerian approaches to curriculum development and evaluation of teaching and student learning. These kinds of instrumentation help the governing bodies feel more in control —give them some trendy crutches to lean on. They tend to be worshipped as ends, not means—to be viewed as tidy panaceas for all school and school system ills. Actually they succeed mainly in angering the people the school system is designed to help because they are seen as mechanistic, unintelligible, and inhumane.

Thus, in many ways the activities of school systems create a heavy burden for local schools to bear—when they touch the schools at all. Often school district administrators are simply divorced from what is happening at school and spend most of their time talking to themselves or criticizing and rewriting reports. Meanwhile, decision making for the school system is immobilized, and educational statesmanship becomes a lost art. As Ellen Goodman has so poignantly remarked, we are faced with "a meltdown of trust" at all levels of operation.

What, then, can be done before the whole operation either blows up or dies of its own weight? According to this observer, the major problems are size, overload (too many new functions and programs piled on top of old ones), misuse of power and technological tools, and misplaced decision making. It is time that we recognize the integrity and importance of the local school as a unit. It is time that we give administration, educational decision making, and power (over budget and personnel selection) back to the school and the community it serves, with only some minor safeguards with respect to equalization of funds and teacher qualifications. It is time that we turn the government of schools upside down and let the local community live with its own triumphs and mistakes. It is time that we create a new institution either to pick up the task of delivery of health and social welfare services to children or to focus on the traditional intellectual and aesthetic goals of the school.

This is not a simple task. Nor can it be accomplished overnight. Long-range planning is essential, as are step-by-step approaches and careful documentation of successful case studies and of failures. This is not a call for a nostalgic return to the little red schoolhouse or for a resurrection of the storefront schools of the 60's. Education for living in our complicated and interdependent world is complex and requires specialized knowledge, skills, and resources not even imagined in the "olden days." Schools cannot and should not be isolated entities. They must have access to resources and talents not available within the confines of the school itself. New designs are needed.

But more important than new designs is the re-education of professionals and community leaders to assume more local autonomy. The fact of the matter is that local schools and communities do not know how to govern themselves. Nor do many of them want to. Further, specialists at the central office and state levels do not really know how to offer technical assistance other than to give commands and write guidelines. There is *much* work to be done.

But it is time to begin. We must find a new recipe for glue to hold local institutions together. We must build a new sense of trust to replace that which has melted down.

REFERENCE

1. *The Washington Post,* January 26, 1980. p. A13.

CHAPTER 16

Leadership, Educational Change, and the Politicalization of American Education

Wendell M. Hough
and Ronald V. Urick

As one looks back over the 60's and 70's, the results of organized efforts in those 20 years to bring about substantive improvements in the education of the nation's children and youth are certainly unremarkable. A review of hundreds of evaluations of federally funded programs has led to serious questions about the usefulness of federal efforts to encourage positive changes in schools and about the prospects for educational reform more generally.[1] The observation that few educators responsible for bringing about changes in schools had an understanding of the process involved is probably still valid today.[2] But it no longer need be so.

In a study conducted by Berman and McLaughlin, several key variables associated with successful change were identified. The high morale of teachers, the active support of principals who appear to be the "gatekeepers" of change, the support of the superintendent and district officials, and the teachers' willingness to spend extra effort were cited as increasing the chances of success.[3] We believe that these findings support the proposition that the school building is the largest single unit in which sustained effort to change and improve curriculum and instruction should occur. The people in each building are unique; they provide unique human dynamics and create a school culture that is specific to each situation.

Educational conferences, symposiums, and lectures provide for the acquisition of new ideas, knowledge, and skills, and, indeed, may raise the level of awareness for professional growth. They are not, however, a substitute for in-service education for the staff of a building that should be the primary locus for professional development and curriculum improvement. To the extent that educational change agents in the 80's begin to address this proposition in their plans and designs for curriculum change or staff development, a significant advance will have been made.

A PROCESS MODEL FOR BUILDING-LEVEL EDUCATIONAL CHANGE

While a building-level focus for educational change is a necessary condition for success, it is not sufficient. The following principles can provide guidance to curriculum workers and staff development specialists as they work to improve the quality of educational experiences for children and youth:

1. Every person is logical in his/her own context.

2. Persons who are to be affected by decisions should be involved in making decisions. Shared decision making builds personal and collective commitment for those involved.

3. The most critical variable in teaching effectiveness is the extent to which one can interact effectively with and release the potential of others.

4. Effective curriculum change is a human process, necessitating change in interaction patterns—e.g., support systems.

5. The principal cannot create effective change, but he/she can block change. The principal can and must facilitate change.

6. Leadership cannot be assumed; any change model should provide a leadership training component.

7. Outside intervention is necessary for significant change in teacher behavior, and feedback on behavior is necessary in order for teachers to understand the impact of their behavior.

8. Although consultant help is necessary and important, direction for change should come from local sources.

163

These principles provide the framework for the conceptualization of a school improvement model that has a proven track record of accomplishment.[4] The model, which is rigorously prescriptive in adhering to these principles, is composed of six steps. They are described in the discussion below.

Step 1: Determination of Needs and Establishment of Priorities

After an interest in or a need for a staff development program has been expressed by a school staff, the principal arranges for a presentation to explain the process to the entire staff. The role and responsibilities of all to be involved—personnel building planning committee and district policy board—are reviewed and explained. Additional time may be spent with the local building staff as needed to determine their level of awareness and readiness for dealing with the staff development process.

Subsequently, an interactive needs assessment is conducted by an external consultant. The needs assessment allows the staff members, along with parent representatives, to select a priority goal that becomes a guide in formulating a proposal to deal with the staff's primary need.

During the needs assessment session, the building staff and parent representatives do the following:

1. Agree on a primary need.

2. Develop the priority goal statement.

3. Participate in activities that will identify forces currently impinging upon the goal.

4. Participate in activities that demonstrate staff commitment to working together to deal with the selected priority goal.

5. Select a committee to write a plan (proposal) that expresses the ideas, needs, and intent of the local staff. This committee remains constant and develops into a leadership team that helps to ensure that the staff development process becomes a built-in continuing change agent at the local building/department level. The structure of this building committee is as follows:
   a. At least two classroom teachers, elected by the teachers
   b. One nonclassroom professional whose position is included in the teachers' contract
   c. Principal
   d. Parent leaders
   e. Staff development facilitator.

Step 2: Proposal Development

The building committee writes the proposal with input and direction from the entire group involved. The proposal must include the following:

1. Statement of the priority goal
2. Statement of the objectives
3. Statement of the strategies
4. Statement of the expected changes
5. Monitoring and evaluation plans/designs
6. Timeliness and schedules
7. Description/identification of resources to be used
8. Cost projections.

Step 3: Proposal Approval

The building staff and community representatives must meet and approve the final proposal before it is transmitted to other groups and to the district policy board for approval. The appropriate fiscal agent is the final approving group.

If any content changes are made or suggested by either the district policy board or the appropriate fiscal agent, the proposal must be returned to the building staff for agreement.

Step 4: Implementation and Development

During the implementation and development stage, a well-structured monitoring and evaluation system must be in operation to ensure that the plan is working. Revisions might occur; if there are major content changes, the proposal, as amended, must go back to the original approving groups. Projects are generally completed within the school year.

Step 5: Monitoring and Evaluation

Monitoring and evaluation procedures, schedules, and designs must be included in the proposal.

The staff development personnel must maintain logs that document progress and record information pertinent to both short-term and long-term monitoring and evaluation for the duration of the project. Various surveys are conducted, and reassessment information is collected and analyzed on a regular basis. From these data, a status report and an evaluative summary are made.

Program planning and evaluation consultants in the area of staff ·development conduct evaluative sessions with the principals and staff development personnel. These sessions result in the development of program recommendations for the following year.

Step 6: Reassessment

When closure is reached on a current proposal, the entire process continues with an interactive reassessment of needs.

POWER AND INFLUENCE IN EDUCATIONAL CHANGE

As the process model described above implies, the teachers and administrators in individual school buildings are highly significant sources of influence in determining the educational outcomes for the students. This has been true in the past and will remain so unless we change dramatically the interface between teacher and learner.

The task of the teacher and the principal, however, is complicated by the impact of broad social forces that are bringing about the politicalization of our school systems to a degree little imagined 20 years ago. Sources of power and influence external to the organizational and professional environments of educators are having increasing impact on curriculum, on patterns of working relationships and authority structures, on testing practices, on teaching methods, and even on the process of change itself.

A recent visitor from a foreign country spent a day in a Michigan public school and noted the following:

1. The school was a junior high school before a federal judge ordered it to be a middle school, causing more than half of the teachers to lose appropriate certification, to say nothing of the impact on the curriculum.

2. Teachers were able to have a duty-free lunch hour because of a collective bargaining agreement.

3. Four teachers were released a half day for in-service training, and substitutes were provided and financed by moneys allocated for staff development by the state legislature.

4. Seventh-grade teachers administered a statewide achievement test as prescribed by the State Department of Education.

5. A consultant from the Intermediate School District (regional educational agency) had a meeting with the principal to discuss

compliance with the federal and state guidelines on mandatory special education.

6. A community advising committee held an afternoon meeting to discuss expenditures of funds from Title I of the Elementary and Secondary Education Act.

7. At lunch time several teachers discussed the consequences of passing or not passing the upcoming millage election.

8. The reading teacher expressed interest in attending next week's conference sponsored by the State Reading Association.

9. A special education teacher made a telephone call to the university to find out what courses she would have to take to become certified in learning disability.

These observations highlight the forces that are influencing the work of our schools. The politics of education has become an agenda item for the courts, state and federal legislative bodies, state departments of education, regional educational agencies, community groups, professional organizations, and schools of education.

The Courts

In recent years the courts have become increasing involved in influencing public education. A startling decision affecting the curriculum and professional staff occurred in Detroit when a federal judge ordered into effect a desegregation plan that involved many programmatic components,[5] including reading and communication skills, vocational education, testing, students' rights and responsibilities, school–community relations, counseling and career guidance, cocurricular activities, bilingual/multiethnic studies, and faculty assignments. Junior high schools were ordered to be middle schools, the creation of five area vocational schools was mandated, and in-service education for all faculty involved in reassignment and/or affected by the transfer of pupils in the desegregation plan was required in the court order. The State of Michigan was required to share equally with the school district in supporting all costs of the implementation of the order. Whether they are addressing issues like prayers in school, due process in discipline cases, or desegregation cases in Louisville (Kentucky), Dayton (Ohio), and Benton Harbor (Michigan), the courts have emerged as central in the formulation of school policy and school curriculum.

Teacher Organizations

A court order can and does have a dramatic and immediate impact on a school system, but the most compelling force influencing the dynamics of schools has been the result of collective bargaining and increasingly powerful education associations. Although wages and working conditions have ostensibly been the primary thrusts of negotiations, there is increasing attention to curriculum and professional development.[6] The Federal Teacher Center legislation that mandated policy boards of 51 percent teachers was quickly followed by the Michigan State Entitlement Program for professional development that required policy boards consisting of 51 percent teachers.[7] Teacher organizations continue to be a strong political force not only in influencing school policy and practices but also in the community at large. In addition, middle management school administrators are now asking for bargaining rights to protect their turf from those above and below them in the bureaucratic structure. More and more decisions that affect school programs today are the result of a series of consultations, if not confrontations, involving the board of education, the superintendent, and various teacher organizations' representatives.

State Legislatures

Spiraling costs for human services are usually subject to only limited discussion in state legislatures. However, debate on education programs and costs generates intense lobbying in most states in the nation. Historically, the education lobbies in some states have not been as influential as some interest groups, but collective bargaining has substantially increased the influence of the entire education community. This community of teacher organizations, administrators, and boards of education may make diverse demands upon the legislative body, but it tends to coalesce behind the demand for dollars for education. While it was once considered beneath the dignity of an educator to exert influence on state legislators, it is now not uncommon for educators to do so, acting collectively.

In response to increased localized pressure, legislators develop categorical aid bills that ultimately affect the funding of all school districts. Just as teachers are including discussion of curriculum matters at the bargaining table, state legislatures are becoming more interested in school programs and professional development. There are indications, once again precipitated and supported by collective bargaining, that involvement in curriculum matters by all levels of educators will be legislated.

State Departments/Boards of Education

The state departments of education, through their spokespersons, the chief state school officers, can have enormous influence both with the state legislatures and through the interpretation of state and federal legislation. State boards can prescribe statewide testing, the number of hours of classroom instruction, and the required courses in teacher preparation programs. The chief state school officer is in a highly politicized position, as are the members of the state board of education. Unlike a local superintendent who frequently finds himself/herself in an adversary situation with the teachers organization or a community group, the chief state school officer can be besieged by multiple groups, each attempting to exert influence and gain support. Constitutionally established to provide education for all youth, state boards of education come into frequent conflict with local boards of education that have tried to maintain their autonomy and control of the educational program.

To monitor the multiplicity of categorical aid programs and the mandates of state boards, the departments of education find it necessary to deploy staff in all sections of their respective states. Decisions with respect to compliance with rules and regulations for special education, bilingual education, compensatory education, vocational education, career education, and the like are all subject to interpretation and to the political process.

Regional Educational Agencies

The governance structure and organization of regional educational agencies vary from state to state, but, in general, they have some regulatory functions as an extension of state departments of education, but are primarily service oriented and consultative. They are competitive for state dollars as well as for possible federal moneys. They constitute a support system for local districts and, as such, can have considerable influence in responding or not responding to the needs of local districts. Federal teacher centers and state entitlement staff development activities are emerging as significant delivery systems in influencing the kind and quality of in-service education. As often as not, the hierarchy of local school districts is not directly involved in decisions on the delivery of service.

Citizens

Although the concept of local control of education has been paramount in the development of the public schools, it was the Elementary and Secondary Act of 1965, Title I, that mandated formal involvement of community advisory groups in the decision-making process of locally developed programs, many of which were operated at the building level. The power and influence of advisory groups vary from just a perfunctory role to one of actually making a compelling judgment on the selection of the building principal.

Concomitant with the increased power of advisory groups has been a tendency for boards of education to become more actively involved in administrative tasks, as distinguished from policy decisions. Increasingly, boards of education are creating their own subcommittees on curriculum, personnel, finance, community relations, and staff development for the purpose of making recommendations to the board for action.

The politics of education is confusing in many ways. There are stabilizing forces, to be sure. For example, leadership people do maintain communication with state legislators as well as congressional representatives and, generally, can expect predictable responses. The same can be said about formally organized civic-oriented organizations. But the makeup of many community pressure groups tends to vary with the issue of the day. They appear unexpectedly with a single mission, usually with considerable volatility and aggressiveness, and eventually disappear, sometimes having taken their toll or possibly having righted a wrong. In any event, school leadership personnel in our society must be responsive to the community.

Professional Organizations

Teacher organizations have led the way so that more and more education professionals have become involved in the politics of education. Resolutions are passed at annual conferences, positions are taken in newsletters, executive directors and organizational leaders become active lobbyists, all in an effort to exert influence on those who make decisions that may affect the membership's concerns and welfare. The very diverse missions of educational organizations tend to present a divided professional education community and, thus, confuse legislators and other policy makers. "When you educators make up your minds on what is best for the school program, we will write the legislation" is not an infrequent response from state legislators.

Colleges of Education

The decline of the K–12 school population has resulted, in turn, in similar declines in the number of students entering colleges of education. Although a plateau as far as size of college faculties may have been reached, the demand for noncredit staff development activities is causing dramatic changes in the way colleges are organized and in the services they deliver. Offices of staff development are becoming common among colleges; state legislatures are drafting legislation for colleges to deliver noncredit activities; and consortia arrangements among local districts, regional educational agencies, and colleges are being formed. These collaborative arrangements are setting the pace for the 80's.

PRODUCTIVE PATTERNS OF LEADERSHIP FOR CHANGE

What are called for, if our schools are to move forward in the 80's, are school leaders, both teachers and administrators, who *understand* the dynamics of organizational life as they relate to the change process, school leaders who *have the skills* required to work effectively in the complex and difficult environment of the 80's described above, school leaders who are *willing* to use that understanding and those skills in the interest of the children and youth who are in their charge.

It is of critical importance to school leaders who seek to bring about significant change that they establish a positive organizational climate. The climate of an organization is a composite of the feelings, attitudes, opinions, and beliefs that members have about the organization, about other members, and about their own role in the organization. There are, according to Olmstead[8], three components of climate that exert extremely powerful effects on organizations: *organizational goals, group relationships, and leadership behavior.*

The important fact about organizational goals is that the motivation to achieve them stems from the individual's involvement with them; thus, when goals are clear, operational, and shared, there is less variation in perceptions regarding optimal courses of action and, hence, less conflict, fewer cross purposes, and less wasted effort.[9]

Group relationships influence the work of a school in at least two ways. First, they influence the motivation of members to perform their tasks; among the motivating properties of group relationships are cohesiveness, trust, and communication.[10] Second, they determine the degree to which staff members come to hold common perceptions regarding school problems.[11]

There are four important elements of leadership behavior that bear directly on the functioning of a school. *Support* refers to the ways in which a principal behaves that enhance the staff's feelings of being

171

worthwhile persons doing worthwhile work. *Team-building* behaviors are those supervisory behaviors that encourage staff members to develop close, mutually satisfying relationships. *Work facilitators* refer to behaviors that organize the work of the staff and assist them in their tasks. *Goal emphasis* behaviors are those that stimulate the staff toward meeting goals and striving for excellence.[12]

These concepts represent the "bottom lines" of understanding, skills, and commitment for school leadership personnel who seek to effect school improvements in the 80's. Support and team-building behaviors provide the means by which school leaders can help themselves and their staff cope with the influences of the external forces described above. Work facilitators and goal emphasis behaviors are the vehicles through which school staffs can be helped to address their *raison d'être:* student learning and growth. These patterns of leadership behaviors, taken together, can build—even in the face of the complexities of the 80's—the kind of organizational climate and staff morale in schools that provide the base for productive change.

By building on the base thus established, by focusing on the school —the largest unit capable of effective change—and by designing a change effort grounded in a sound conceptual base—like the staff development model described above—school leaders in the 80's move our schools forward toward the goals of equality and excellence of education for all our children and youth.

REFERENCES

1. Berman, P., and McLaughlin, M. *Federal Programs Supporting Educational Change, Vol. IV: The Findings in Review.* Santa Monica, Calif.: Rand Corporation, 1975. p. 2.

2. Sarason, Seymour. *The Culture of the School and the Problem of Change.* New York: Allyn & Bacon, 1971.

3. Berman, P., and McLaughlin, M. *op. cit.*

4. The model was conceptualized by the authors and developed and implemented by Geneva Hoover, Director of Staff Development of the Taylor (Michigan) Community Schools, and her staff, 1975–1980.

5. *Ronald Bradley, et al. v. William Milliken, et al.* Civil No. 35257. Memorandum opinion and remedial decree, United States District Court, Eastern District of Michigan, Southern Division, 1975. p. 124.

6. Frock, Arthur C. "The Hidden Determiners: A Trend Study Descriptive of the Extent to Which Language Directly Affecting Curriculum Exists in Teacher Collective Bargaining Agreements in Selected School Districts in Southeastern Michigan." Doctoral Dissertation. Detroit: College of Education, Wayne State University, 1977.

7. School Aid Act of 1979.

8. Olmstead, J.A. "Organizational Factors in the Performance of Social Welfare and Rehabilitation Workers." *Working Papers, No. 1. National Study of Social Welfare and Rehabilitation Workers, Work, and Organizational Contexts.* U.S. Department of Health, Education, and Welfare, Social and Rehabilitation Services (SRS), 72-05402. Washington, D.C.: U.S. Government Printing Office, 1971.

9. Katz, D., and Kahn, R.L. *The Social Psychology of Organizations.* New York: John C. Wiley, 1966.

Olmstead, J.A. *op. cit.*

Likert, R., and Likert, J.G. *New Ways of Managing Conflict.* New York: McGraw-Hill Book Co., 1976.

10. Likert, R., and Likert, J.G. *op. cit.*

11. Olmstead, J.A. *op. cit.*

12. Franklin, J.L.; Wissler, A.L.; and Spencer, G.J. *Survey-Guided Development III: A Manual for Concepts Training.* Revised edition. La Jolla, Calif.: University Associates, 1977.

Likert, R., and Likert, J.G. *op. cit.*

Part V

THE UNFINISHED AGENDA

What all this means for us is that we should neither be optimistic nor pessimistic, but possibilist . . . .

. . . a new bird will have to be found to symbolize American education—the parrot and psittacotic method of teaching will no longer be appropriate.

Ole Sand

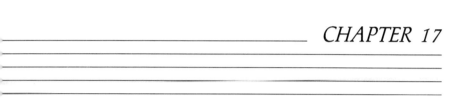

CHAPTER 17

The Unfinished Agenda

Robert M. McClure

Twenty years ago, at the outset of Ole Sand's distinguished career with the National Education Association, his Project on Instruction published *Schools for the Sixties,* [1] the first of a four-volume series that would make a number of bold propositions about the future of schooling in America. A few came to pass; most did not.

The predictions of other well-reasoned studies of those heady days suffered similar fates. Several essays in this book point to the reasons. In the general society there were, for example, radical and unforeseen demographic changes; a war that had wrenching effects on the values of the American people; a conservative, if not a right-wing, backlash to the effects of that war; and the jolt taken by the American economy because of the energy crisis. In addition, forces that more directly shaped the nature of schooling were also at work: the ascendancy of the behavioral psychologists and their impact on decision making, the tendency toward centralizing school functions, the decline of the number of students in schools, the role television plays in affecting patterns of student behavior, the real or artificially created decline of public confidence in school quality, and the increased influence of the courts, the federal government, and teacher organizations.

Those who had the opportunity to work in schools in the 60's and to still be around them in the 80's might conclude that the world of the school is entirely different, that the agendas have changed. In some measure that is true because our society and our children have changed in some remarkable ways during the last 20 years, and we now have increased knowledge about learning and teaching that was not available two decades ago. But, as our contributors observe, the essential tasks of keeping school remain—developing literacy, helping to create responsible citizens, preparing students for the world of work, and achieving self-realization.

The forces that have caused schools to become what they are today —and most particularly the expanding of access to an education—are going to be with us in the decade ahead. The stance taken in this essay, however, is that there will be substantial shifts in the nature of those forces and that considerations of both equity and excellence will be in the forefront. For example, attention will continue to be given to the desegregation of the public schools, but that will be coupled with stronger pushes toward increasing the quality of opportunities for students. "What happens at the end of the bus ride" will become as much a concern as the attempt to find satisfactory methods to ensure racial equality.

Two basic issues related to equity and excellence will give direction to the work of educators and policy makers in the 80's. The first is to determine the ways to strengthen the public schools, to regain the confidence of the American public, to make the schools more central to and pervasive in the affairs of our democracy. The second, really an integral part of the first, is to more clearly define quality in the schools. This essay, written on behalf of the Ole Sand Memorial Fund Committee, examines some possible agendas for the schools during the decade. Propositions are made concerning several topics: purposes, objectives, inclusion/exclusion, content organization, materials, standards, assessment of student progress, and school improvement processes. The sixteen essays that precede this one, as well as other material—and particularly the *Schools for the Sixties* and *Schools for the Seventies* series—have been used extensively in developing these propositions.

One contributor reminds us that Ole Sand thought one mark of a good school was the emergence of a belly laugh from classrooms every once in awhile. He was concerned that schools be not funereal but alive with the sounds of purpose—one of which was to gain a perspective on the affairs of humankind, and that meant a dose of humor in the process. One wonders what Ole would have thought of the so-called back-to-the-basics movement with its mechanistic, passionless view of curriculum, teachers, and students. Humor notwithstanding, there are in today's schools too few opportunities for students to have real and substantial engagement with important ideas that ought to be at the heart of the curriculum. Increasingly, curricular decisions are made on the basis of ease of measurement of outcomes rather than on the worth of the content.

For several decades, emphasis in the American school curriculum has shifted with the times. In the 30's, the heyday of progressivism, the needs of the child were emphasized. Later, when the country was engaged in a war that enjoyed the support of the people, the needs of society became paramount. In the 50's, when the Cold War was in full swing and competition with the Russians was uppermost, the schools turned to the academicians for a scholarly renewal of the curriculum, with particular emphasis on science and mathematics programs. Later, during the 60's, when the Vietnam War and Woodstock were causing us to seek "relevance," the schools moved away from a common curriculum to a proliferation of electives and a different view of standards. In the 70's, as Goodlad says in his essay, "the back-to-basics movement has spoken to diminished curricular expectations. . . ."

In the 80's the American school curriculum should avoid the swing of the pendulum, and greater attention should be paid to the substantial amount of information now available to us about good schooling. Excesses, imbalance, and nescient attitudes about our history should be avoided; data about human growth and development, learning processes, the potential needs of students and society in the future, and organized knowledge should be considered more often in planning and implementing the curriculum. Planning processes that attend to these essentials will produce a school program for the 80's significantly different from those of the past.

PURPOSES

The movement of the 80's to reinstate a common body of knowledge for students to acquire is consistent with what is known about good education. That common body of knowledge, however, must be truly germane to the present and future needs of students and society; therefore, it must be carefully selected. What must be avoided is the insistence that all students acquire their schooling in precisely the same way, that specific outcomes within the major purposes be the same for each, and that certain skills or knowledge in the curriculum be valued more highly than others.

Those who will establish the purposes of schooling will be forced to choose from a variety of historical precedents but to interpret them in the context of a new age. It seems very likely, for example, that a central function of the school will be to develop literacy. That goal, however, will be pushed not only toward universality but also toward an expanded definition of literacy. Such a new definition will undoubtedly include the ability to distinguish propaganda, to think critically, to read messages other than verbal or written, and to use the language more richly and fully. It also seems likely that as we expand the definition of literacy, we will require competency in more than one language. Similarly, computational skills will continue to be a focus, but teachers and other curriculum makers will expand the definition of competency to include a thorough familiarity with mathematical systems, an appreciation of the elegance of those systems, and an understanding of what mathematical machines can do in helping to solve problems.

If we are to take our recent history of schooling seriously, however, a common body of knowledge for all students will include more than the classic duo of language and mathematics. The 80's will see a return to an emphasis on skills, attitudes, and knowledge related to the individual's role in a participatory democracy. The decade will also see a resurgence of the visual and performing arts, and their playing a central role in a curriculum common to all. More attention will be paid to understanding our history and that of others, and to developing attitudes that help graduates accept and value those whose heritage is different. The basic fundamentals of the physical, natural, and social sciences will become more central rather than being reserved for those aspiring to college admission. And in these offerings students will learn more about fundamental operations so as to become more enlightened decision makers in the complex affairs of our society. More attention will be given to helping students be analytical about themselves, particularly as that self-knowledge relates to making important decisions about occupations and life-styles.

More in the realm of process than substance, it will also be important that each student select a field of study and achieve psychological ownership of it. For some that will be aerodynamics, for others the guitar, and for others a sport. The subject will matter less than the opportunity for the learner to acquire the skills of inquiry, the discipline of perseverance, and the satisfactions of mastery. The adoption of such a purpose would do much to help students have the skills, inclinations, and attitude to become lifelong learners.

Curriculum developers in the 80's will have to make some very tough decisions about the core curriculum for all students. It is an

180

essential task because the role that schooling is to play in the education of children and youth is now becoming too diffuse. Many believe that the school has had to take on more responsibilities than it is prepared to competently fulfill. The range of central purposes should be limited to those that the school is able to achieve.

That is not to say, however, that the school should not serve purposes other than those selected by it as central for all students. The opportunity, for example, to develop job-related skills is certainly a school-related purpose, but it is one that will vary greatly from student to student and that requires the participation of other institutions. Purposes related to recreation or to health are other examples that call for programs jointly planned and implemented by the school and other agencies in the community.

A school's curricular purposes comprise a value statement that defines that school's view of a liberally educated person. The suggestions made in this section and elsewhere are those of an individual and are made without reference to a particular student or student body. In other sections, attention will be paid to processes for curricular decision making and implementation that are built on student, citizen, and professional involvement.

OBJECTIVES

To suggest that there is a common set of curricular purposes for all students is not to say that there are common objectives for all. Our recent experience with Individualized Education Programs (IEPs) for handicapped students indicates that the profession is ready to take some steps to individualize not only instruction but also the curriculum for students. True curricular individualization is going to be difficult, though, since we are just beginning to acquire the practical experience necessary for this complex task. Attempts at individualization in the past have been chiefly guided by rate of learning, not by attention to other variables.

In the future, when IEPs are common for all students, objectives will describe the various routes that individuals can take to acquire the desired learning. Thus, on the road to computational literacy, one student's program for a period of time will emphasize a theoretical orientation while another's will stress application.

Developing individual curricular objectives for students calls for using the skills and judgments of teachers in making short- and long-range decisions. School-systemwide objectives will become more generic, and those closest to the learner will be called upon to develop objectives to give specific guidance to the instructional and learning processes. Since purposes and objectives should be directed toward the most significant of content, there will be less emphasis on quantitative indicators ("correctly identify 80 out of 100") of achievement. The ability to make sound judgments about the nature of objectives for particular students and to accurately assess progress toward those objectives will be among the chief skills of the teacher of the 80's.

INCLUSION/EXCLUSION

Deciding what to include in the curriculum is the most difficult and important decision of curriculum makers. Surely, at one time it was easier when knowledge was more static, and there was little argument about what was valued. Today, new knowledge is produced at an astonishing rate, and there is considerable societal conflict about questions of curricular inclusion and exclusion. To avoid the potentially devastating effects of a fight in the community over a curriculum offering, school policy makers settle for blandness and the status quo. Too often, the result is students who are bored because they know, or at least sense, that their program has no relevance to their present or future.

It is difficult to know how the schools will be able to begin to make some tough and rational decisions about what should be learned in school in today's charged political atmosphere. Certainly the emergence of a leadership group with political strength, rationality, and integrity would be in order. There are some signs that an amalgamation of parents and teachers will take shape that could set some bold directions for the reform of the school curriculum.

If the public school is to continue to be a force for constructive growth, enlightenment, and strong participatory democracy, several criteria should guide the choices of curriculum makers. Six such criteria proposed in *Schools for the Sixties* remain relevant today:

1. Is it learning that is based substantially upon bodies of organized knowledge, such as the arts and sciences?

2. Is it learning of complex and difficult things that requires organization of experience and distribution of practice over long periods of time?

3. Is it learning in which the essential factors must be brought specially to the attention of the learner? For example, concepts that explain the growth of plants are not obvious to an observer of plants.

4. Is it an experience that cannot be provided directly in the ordinary activities of daily living?

5. Is it learning that requires a more structured experience than is usually available in life outside the school?

6. Is it learning that requires reexamination and interpretation of experience?[2]

In addition to these criteria, two others will be important for curriculum policy makers in the 80's. The first is to define as carefully as possible the basic knowledge and skills necessary for all graduates. This will be particularly critical in regard to language, citizenship, and critical-thinking skills.

It will also be important to avoid the tendency to overprescribe and, in so doing, to insist on a greater number of common learnings than are truly germane to the education of all individuals. Thus, a second consideration has to do with the potential for the intended learning to be useful in the future life of the student. Skills in predicting such future occurrences as the nature of jobs or the kinds of social problems that will be with us are improving, and these tools should be increasingly utilized by policy makers and curriculum developers.

CONTENT ORGANIZATION

Students of the 80's will be citizens, jobholders, and members of a society in the year 2000 and beyond—an age that will be very different from today. The way in which organized knowledge is conceptualized and used will be as different then as is now from what it was a hundred years ago. To continue to narrowly compartmentalize curricular content, as has been the practice of the 70's, may inhibit youngsters' abilities to generalize, see productive relationships, or be effective solvers of complex problems.

A fundamental task of curriculum developers in the 80's will be to help school faculties organize curricular purposes so that students deepen their understandings over time, add to their range of knowledge and skills, and see significant relationships across the curriculum. Our experience with "magnet schools," in which the essentials are taught chiefly through one discipline, is giving us some practical ways to organize content so that it more accurately reflects our purposes. Problem-centered curriculums, certain forms of team teaching, a few textbook ventures, and some different manifestations of cross-discipline departmentalization now in place in a few schools will provide teachers, principals, and curriculum workers with other needed experience.

183

MATERIALS

The curriculum process literature clearly indicates that teacher in-service education and the provision of curriculum-specific materials for students are two of the most important variables in effecting lasting change. The kind of widespread reform suggested for the 80's in several of these essays will take firm hold only when the materials of instruction support it.

If the propositions made here become practice, however, the source, nature, and organization of instructional materials will vary from those presently in use. If, for example, the development and implementation of learner objectives become the domain of the building faculty, teacher teams, and individual teachers, then those professionals must have an increased role in the development of these instructional resources. Certainly not all instructional materials can or should be homegrown because such a practice would deny students the vast resources that American publishers can provide them. However, state and even local sanctioning of texts and other resources as the only avenue of getting materials into the schools should not continue to be practice. No one in a state department of education or a school system central office can judge the appropriateness of a given set of materials when students' instructional programs are individually tailored. Teachers need a vast array of materials available to them to support the objectives and procedures that they have established with their learners.

No such storehouse can ever contain all of the materials needed to help students achieve the objectives appropriate for them. Building faculties will need to develop the skills to specify the nature of the materials specific to their curricular intentions. School-based materials specialists, teacher aides, and volunteers should also receive special training so that the faculty's specifications can be carried out.

It would be better for our schools, teachers, and students if decisions about instructional materials could be apolitical, less subject to the influences of special interest groups. That has, however, never been the case in American education, and thus far in the 80's, the situation appears dismal. For example, legislation is pending in several states that forces textbook publishers to discount scientific theories of evolution and to treat a literal and fundamentalist interpretation of the Bible on matters of creation as fact. By omission or deliberate slanting, other knowledge is badly treated in textbooks. There is, for example, little or no treatment of the American labor movement in textbooks, and there is still a dearth of information available in instructional materials about the contributions of blacks to the American culture. The academic scholars would do well to turn their attention to this issue and to speak out, with concerned teachers and parents, for textbooks and other materials that are more thoroughly grounded in fact and enlightened thought.

STANDARDS

American educators, spurred on by the significant research of Benjamin Bloom and others, have been inching toward acceptance of the concept of mastery as the standard against which to judge achievement. The major conditions for student mastery—time and opportunities— have not been available heretofore in our lock-step system of schooling. That should change in the 80's.

Webster's Third New International Dictionary defines *mastery* as "the skill or knowledge in a subject that makes one a master of it." To be masterful of punctuation, for example, one must understand and be able to apply the standardized signs in a consistently correct fashion. If the student's objective is to learn basic photographic skills, but she or he is allowed to proceed without knowing how to completely control a camera's aperture and shutter speeds, then the objective cannot be reached. Or if a youngster is to acquire the skills necessary to make reasoned judgments about the qualities of paintings, a fundamental understanding of chromatics is essential. Sometimes knowing how or understanding and sometimes not is insufficient; only a complete understanding will do.

One spur to the growing acceptance of mastery as a standard has been the realization that the cutoff scores on tests used to implement accountability programs are nonsensical. These scores are almost always established without regard to any conceptual view of competency. Seemingly out of the air comes a pronouncement that "7 out of 10" or "80 out of 100" is sufficient to demonstrate that a student has enough knowledge to perform adequately or to move on to more advanced work. If we have paid sufficient attention to questions of inclusion/exclusion in making curricular decisions, then such artificially set levels of acceptance are inappropriate. Something is either worth knowing or doing or valuing, or it is not.

The problem is that our system sets a standard of "a year's growth in a year" and does not permit attention to be paid a number of variables that significantly affect learners' ability to acquire new information or skills. Accepting mastery as the standard against which to measure student achievement requires that schools be organized in ways that offer students a variety of routes by which to become masterful, that provide sufficient instructional resources to support multiple learning opportunities, and that allow the time necessary for each learner to become fully competent in an area of study.

ASSESSMENT OF STUDENT PROGRESS

Perhaps no movement in American education has been more damaging to the achievement of the truly important purposes of schooling than has the effort to overly quantify objectives and their measurement. Breaking content down into small and almost meaningless parts, assuming sequentialness without supporting data, and basing achievement almost exclusively on paper-and-pencil tests prepared far away from the learning site produce students who are not equipped to deal with a complex world. It is the industrial model badly misapplied to a uniquely human enterprise. Our scientific measurement skills are not as great as policy makers believe. Yet, too many curriculum decisions today are dictated by this less-than-adequate science.

Educators must take much of the responsibility for this unhappy state of affairs since we were the ones who nurtured the public's faith in standardized achievement tests and in many of the ill-conceived accountability schemes now in effect. We have the ideas, expertise, commitment, and resources, however, to develop more suitable and humane processes and procedures to assess student growth. A number of characteristics of good assessment procedures are referred to in other essays.[3] Since student assessment became such a crucial issue in the 70's and will likely remain so in the 80's, it is imperative that these ideas be explored and put more widely into practice.

SCHOOL IMPROVEMENT PROCESSES

Many important decisions about schooling in the 70's were made at levels that were a considerable distance from learners and their teachers. In large measure these decisions did not contribute to the vitality of the learning and teaching enterprise. A reversal of that trend is in order.

Key to improving the processes of reform is the development of the school building faculty to help it become more central in decision making about curriculum and instruction. Clearly, this group of professionals knows more about its students and their community than anyone else. With the proper support, effective staff development programs, and the authority and freedom to act delegated by enlightened boards of education, a school faculty could plan and deliver programs of exceptionally high quality.

A faculty confident of its abilities to effect constructive change would create meaningful ways to involve students, parents, and others in the community in the significant decisions about the program of the school. Tokenism would give way to true and appropriate participation in the affairs of the school by its clients.

It is proposed, in short, that many of the decisions discussed in this essay—decisions about objectives, organization of content, selection and preparation of materials, definitions of competency, and methods to assess student progress—are best left to those closest to where learning occurs.

Harold Gores, founder of the Educational Facilities Laboratory and a frequent contributor of ideas to NEA's *Schools for the Sixties* program, liked to use a "from–to" format in suggesting directions for the future. Ole liked the format and practically made an art form of it in his speeches and writing—for example:

FROM	TO
memory	inquiry
spiritless climate	zest for learning
classrooms that are like kitchens	classrooms that are like libraries and living rooms[4]

It is appropriate to conclude this book with a new series of from–to's in the Gores/Sand tradition—a road map, if you will, of our view of directions for the 80's:

FROM	TO
centralized decision making	decision making by those closest to the learners
smatterings of knowledge	mastery
a diffuse curriculum	a curriculum that is targeted
subjects within a course of study unrelated to each other	a unified approach stressing interrelationships
materials not curriculum-specific to individual students	instructional materials drawn from a wide variety of sources including large numbers designed specifically for individuals or small groups

| the same learning opportunities for all | a wide variety of opportunities leading toward similar purposes |
| a sterile learning environment | a learning environment that is aesthetically satisfying and matched to curricular and instructional purposes |

REFERENCES

1. *Schools for the Sixties: Report of the NEA Project on Instruction.* New York: McGraw-Hill Book Company, Inc., 1963. Other books in the series are *Deciding What To Teach, Education in a Changing Society,* and *Planning and Organizing for Teaching.* Washington, D.C.: National Education Association, 1963.

2. *Ibid.* pp. 33–34.

3. For other suggestions, see: Quinto, Frances, and McKenna, Bernard. *Alternatives to Standardized Testing.* Washington, D.C.: National Education Association, 1977.

4. Sand, Ole. *On Staying Awake: Talks With Teachers.* Washington, D.C.: National Education Association, 1970. pp. 36–37.

Cordell Affeldt is president of the Indiana State Teachers Association and has served on numerous NEA committees. She has taught 16 years in public and private elementary schools in California, Wisconsin, and Indiana. She has also taught at Ball State University in Muncie, Indiana.

James A. Banks is Professor of Education at the University of Washington. Professor Banks is a specialist in social studies education, ethnic studies, and multiethnic education. His books include _Teaching Strategies for the Social Studies, Teaching Strategies for Ethnic Studies, Teaching Ethnic Studies: Concepts and Strategies,_ and _Multiethnic Education: Theory and Practice._ He edited the NEA publication _Education in the 80's: Multiethnic Education._

Lois V. Edinger is Professor of Education at the University of North Carolina at Greensboro. She served as president of the National Education Association, 1964–1965, and as chairperson of the Advisory Committee, Center for the Study of Instruction, NEA, 1969–1971. Professor Edinger is a specialist in social studies education and intercultural/global education.

Geneva Gay is Associate Professor of Education at Purdue University. She is currently a member of the Editorial Board of the _Phi Delta Kappan._ Dr. Gay consults nationwide with educational institutions and agencies on staff preparation and curriculum development for multicultural education. Her publications include more than 45 journal articles and book chapters.

John I. Goodlad is Dean of the Graduate School of Education and Director of the Laboratory in School and Community Education at UCLA. In addition, he is Director of Research for the Institute for Development of Educational Activities, Inc., an affiliate of the Charles F. Kettering Foundation. He is author or co-author of 20 books, including most recently, _The Dynamics of Educational Change_ (1975), _Facing the Future: Issues in Education and Schooling_ (1976), _Curriculum Inquiry: The Study of Curriculum Practice_ (1979), and _What Schools Are For_ (1979).

Margaret Gill Hein, Executive Director and co-founder of Business and Industry for the Arts in Education, Inc. (BIFAE), was Executive Secretary of the Association for Supervision and Curriculum Development for six years. She has been Head, Department of Teacher Education, Mills College, and Associate Dean, School of Education, Lehigh University. She has contributed to journals and books and consults with schools and organizations, especially those working on curriculum development and the study of teaching/learning.

Wendell M. Hough is Associate Dean and Professor of Administrative and Organizational Studies in the College of Education, Wayne State University. A former Assistant Superintendent for Instruction in metropolitan Detroit, Dr. Hough serves as a staff development consultant to local school systems. He has developed, with Dr. Ronald Urick, an interactive needs assessment procedure which establishes the individual building as the locus for staff development and curriculum improvement.

Robert M. McClure is a Senior Professional Associate with the National Education Association, Instruction and Professional Development. He has served as teacher, curriculum consultant, and curriculum director in the California public schools and was on the staff of UCLA as Associate Director of the Ford Program on the Education of Teachers.

Willard H. McGuire is a former teacher of algebra and Spanish in the Minnesota public schools. After serving as Vice-President of the National Education Association for five years, McGuire was elected President of the Association in 1979. He has served as a delegate to the Assembly of the World Confederation of Organizations of the Teaching Profession, and in 1975 he was chairperson of the NEA delegation to the WCOTP Assembly in Berlin. On NEA's behalf he has consulted with leaders of national teacher organizations in Japan, Israel, Honduras, the Soviet Union, and France.

Bernard McKenna is a program development specialist with the National Education Association where he works in the areas of teacher education and professional standards, professional development, and the evaluation of teaching, student learning progress, and educational programs. His writings include *Staffing the Schools*, "Minimal Competency Testing: The Need for a Broader Context" in *Educational Horizons*, and *Context/Environment Effects in Teacher Evaluation* (in press).

Lois A. Martin is Associate Superintendent for Instruction and Program Development in the Montgomery County (Maryland) Public Schools. In addition to teaching and serving as a high school department head, Dr. Martin has held a variety of line and staff administrative positions in elementary and secondary education. She writes and lectures frequently on sex role stereotyping, instructional improvement, program evaluation, and curriculum development.

Edward J. Meade, Jr., is Program Officer for Education and Public Policy at the Ford Foundation and has been primarily concerned with public education during his 20 years at the Foundation. Dr. Meade also has served as a senior advisor to several U.S. Commissioners of Education, Secretaries of HEW, the Department of Defense, the U.S. Navy, the Federal Communications Commission, and the White House, on education and training programs and policies. He has published widely in popular and professional journals.

W. C. Meierhenry is Professor and Chairperson of Adult and Continuing Education and Professor of Educational Administration, Teachers College, University of Nebraska–Lincoln. Among his recent articles are "Learning and Instructional Theory Revisited" in *American Annals of the Deaf,* "Instructional Theory: From Behaviorism to Humanism to Synergism," in *Instructional Innovator,* and *Lifelong Learning Through Telecommunications.* He received the Distinguished Service Award presented by the Association for Educational Communications and Technology in 1980.

Dorothy V. Meyer is Associate Professor of Education at the University of Lowell. A former secondary school teacher and an education and human services administrator, she has been active in involving citizens in the decision-making process of programs that directly affect them. She has held numerous offices in education associations including that of President of the Massachusetts Teachers Association and Vice-President of the National Council of State Education Associations.

Roland H. Nelson is Professor of Education Administration at the University of North Carolina at Greensboro and Adjunct Program Specialist with the Center for Creative Leadership, Greensboro, North Carolina. He has held various administrative positions in colleges and universities, and most recently served as President of Marshall University. Professor Nelson's primary interest is leadership in bureaucratic organizations. He is co-author with Dale Brubaker of *Creative Survival in Educational Bureaucracies.*

Ralph W. Tyler is Director Emeritus, Center for Advanced Study in the Behavioral Sciences. His professional career has included membership with the faculties of the University of Nebraska, University of North Carolina, Ohio State University, and University of Chicago. He was Director of Evaluation for the Eight-Year Study, 1934–1942; Director of the Cooperative Study in General Education, 1939–1945; Director of the

Examinations Staff of the Armed Forces Institute, 1942–1953; and Chairperson of the Exploratory Committee on Assessing the Progress of American Education. He has been a consultant on curriculum development to many institutions in the United States and abroad.

Ronald V. Urick is Professor of Administrative and Organizational Studies in the College of Education, Wayne State University. A specialist in staff development, Professor Urick has served as consultant to schools, colleges and universities, as well as to government agencies at the state and national levels. He is co-developer of the ARC (Awareness, Readiness, Commitment) model of staff development and is the author of *Alienation: Individual or Social Problem?*

Elizabeth C. Wilson has had a long career in administration, supervision, curriculum development, and teacher education in both public and independent schools. She now works as a consultant in curriculum and instruction for a variety of educational projects sponsored by such agencies as the Alban Institute; the School of Education, Lowell University; the National Public Radio; and the Agency for Instructional Television. Dr. Wilson frequently contributes to educational journals and books.